AF497303

Registers

of

BROAD CHALKE,

CO. WILTS.

Registers

OF

Broad Chalke,

CO. WILTS,

FROM 1538 TO 1780.

EDITED BY

THE REV. CECIL GURDEN MOORE, M.A.,

VICAR.

PRIVATELY PRINTED.

EIGHTY COPIES (FOR SUBSCRIBERS ONLY).

LONDON:
MITCHELL AND HUGHES, PRINTERS, 140 WARDOUR STREET, W.
1881.

PREFACE.

THE* parish of Broad Chalke is in the Hundred of Chalke, the ^{Grant in} greater part of which was granted in 955 by King Eadwic to ^{A.D. 955.} the nuns of Wilton, and described as Ceolcan.

The two parishes of Broad and Bower Chalke are surveyed ^{Mention} in Domesday Book under the name of Chelche. ^{in 'Domes-day Book.'}

In 'Testa de Nevill' it is stated that the Abbess of Wilton ^{In 'Testa} held Villam de Chalke *in capite* of our Lord the King, and that ^{de Nevill.'} it was the chief manor of her barony. Also that Robert Maskarel held a knight's fee in Girardston of the said Abbess; that Joan de Nevill held half a knight's fee in Knighton of the said Abbess; and that Rois de Verdun held the vill of Stoke in socage of the Abbess.

As these three sub-divisions of the parish, together with another called Moulsell, are occasionally mentioned in the Registers, I proceed to give a brief account of their early history.

1. Girardston, *vulgo* Guston, was held, at the time of the ^{Girard-} completion of Domesday Book, by Girard. A lineal descendant ^{ston.} of his was a Gerard living 12th Henry II., who assumed the name of De Chelcha of Chalk Parva; his daughter married Robert de Maskarel, who thus came into possession of the estate, as mentioned in 'Testa de Nevill.' The Marria Maskerell of the Marriage Register for 1563 was, probably, a member of this family.

The still older name of Girard may possibly be traced in the ^{Name of} variously spelt entries of Gerret, Garret, Gerard, Gerrard, Jered, ^{Girard} and Jeret, and if so, that race has one descendant still repre- ^{still exist-} senting it in the parish. ^{ing.}

2. The hamlet of Knighton, anciently, and still a manor, ^{Knighton.} was included in the before-mentioned grant by King Eadwic to the nuns of Wilton.

The half-knight's fee held here by Joan de Nevill descended ^{Joan de} from her to the Saint Martins, and afterwards to the families ^{Nevill's} of Lord Lovell, Sir Roger Caleston, and the Darells. In 38 ^{estate.}

* Abridged from Bowles's Hundred of Chalk in Hoare's 'History of Wiltshire.' London, 1838.

Henry VIII. it was the property of Sir Edward Darell, and shortly after appears to have been bought by the Earl of Pembroke, in possession of whose descendant it remains.

Alan's or Alwyn's estate.

Besides this estate, there were lands in Knighton belonging to Alan or Alwyn, connected with the Alans or Fitzalans, Earls of Arundel. This John Alan had licence from Edward II. to

Chantry founded.

found a chantry or chapel to the honour of God and All Saints.* This was in existence from its foundation, in 1322, until the dissolution of chantries, in the beginning of the reign of Edward VI. It was on the south side of the church, and is still called the Knighton aisle. The property given for the maintenance of the chantry priest appears to have been granted to the Saint Loe family, whose name is frequently mentioned in the Registers, but is now extinct. The rest of the Alan property belonged, at various periods, to the Le Despencers, Paynells, Dukes of Gloucester, Earls of Arundel, and finally to the Earls of Pembroke.

Stoke Verdon.

3. Stoke, Stoke Verdon, or Stoke Farthing, is also a manor. It was formerly the seat of the Lords de Verdon. Rois de Verdon, who held it at the date of the 'Testa de Nevill,' was foundress of the Monastery of Grace Dieu, in Leicestershire, and afterwards married Theobald de Botiller, who took his wife's name of Verdon. The last male representative of this family died in 1316, since which time the Barony has remained in abeyance. The estate then went to Lord Furnival, who had married the eldest daughter.

Comes to Earl of Shrewsbury.

In 1406 it came, by marriage, into the possession of Lord Talbot, afterwards created Earl of Shrewsbury. He was killed while commanding the English forces in France, 20 July, 1453, and among the titles inscribed on his tomb at Rouen is that of "Lord Verdon of Acton." In the reign of Henry VIII. the property came into possession of the Earls of Pembroke, who still own it.

Moulsell. Family of Gawen.

4. Mouse-hill, Mount Sorrell, or Moulsell, was formerly part of the possessions of the family of Gawen, of which Aubrey, in his 'Miscellanies,' published in 1721, says, that they had owned this property for 450 years, and perhaps more. Tradition tells us that the Gawens were descended from Gawain or Gawyn, sister's son of King Arthur.

Estate of the Penruddockes and Aubreys.

The principal estate of Broad Chalke, with mansion house, etc., was leased, for many years, from the Earls of Pembroke by the Penruddockes; subsequently by the Aubreys. On an old

---

* The Parish Church is dedicated to All Saints.

beam, now in the belfrey of the church, is the following inscription:—" This church repaired and the five bells made six, ano 1629. G. Penruddocke and John Aubrey Esq^{res} Churchwardens."

This John Aubrey was the well-known historian, or archæologist who died at Oxford, and was buried there in 1697.

The Registers here printed are contained in seven parts : *The Registers.*

1. Old Vellum book,
    a. Baptisms 1588—1653.
    b. Marriages 1562—1649.
    c. Burials 1552—1653.
2. Parchment sheet,
    "Register of the Births," 1653—1658.
3. Four parchment sheets,
    a. Burials 1660—1676.
    b. Baptisms 1700—1722.
4. Paper Register,
    a. Burials 1677—1716.
    b. Ditto 1720—1782.

Certificates of Burials in Woollen are entered from 25 September, 1677, to 29 November, 1770.

5. Nineteen leaves of vellum,
    Baptisms 1723—1802.
6. Two leaves of vellum,
    Marriages 1725—1754.
7. Printed Register,
    Marriages 1754—1801.

From this it will appear that the Registers for the following years are missing, viz. :— *Missing Registers.*

    Baptisms 1659—1700 = 41 years.
    Marriages 1650—1725 = 75 years.
    Burials 1654—1660 = 6 years.
    Ditto 1716—1720 = 4 years.

The general destination of missing Registers seems to have been to be sold to lace-makers.

I have endeavoured to supply the gap caused by the carelessness of some of my predecessors by a careful search in the Sarum Diocesan Registry, the results of which will be found printed as an Appendix. *Search in Diocesan Registry.*

The earliest volume is in very good preservation, though some entries are illegible from the fading of the ink.

I have followed the self-evident incorrect spelling in such of the entries as have clearly been left to the care of a parish clerk.

Two instances of the way in which family names get changed *Gradual change of names.*

from what they originally were, either by a mere contraction, or by being spelt according to popular pronunciation, may here be cited.

Fox-hanger. The name of Foxhanger (misprinted as Foxganger) appears in the Marriage Register for 1618, and on various subsequent occasions, but in 1629 it will be seen that two children of an Edward Foxhanger are called simply Foxe, and in 1631, both child and father are described as Fox.

The other instance is a more remarkable one. In the Baptismal Register for 1540 there appears the name of John **Yellow.** Yelow; in the Marriage Register for 1609, Christopher Eilfe marries Jane Randoll.

In the Baptisms for 1611, there is the following entry:—Jane Eilffe d. Christopher Eilffe, but in the original MS. the name Yellow is first written, in each case, and then struck through and Eilffe written above. In 1615, 1619, and 1622 this same Christopher has his surname spelt in three different ways,—1st, Yelfes; 2nd, Yellowes; and 3rd, Yelf. There must have been something very peculiar in the common pronunciation of this name which could render possible such different versions of it in writing.

Surviving Families. The Families mentioned in the Registers more than 300 years ago, which still have representatives in the parish, are the following:—

Langtree, first mentioned in Baptismal Register,			1588.
King,	ditto	ditto	1589.
Golden,	ditto	ditto	1541.
Selwood,	ditto	ditto	1542.
Pen(n)y,	ditto	ditto	1550.
Witte,	ditto	ditto	1551.
Shergall,	ditto	ditto	1552.
Scammell,	ditto	ditto	1562.
Gerret,	ditto	ditto	1569.
Francis,	ditto	ditto	1573.
Barter,	ditto	ditto	1577.
Humby,	ditto	ditto	1579.

General particulars. The parish of Broad Chalke had 811 inhabitants by the Census of 1871. It contains very nearly 7000 acres. The living is a Vicarage in the gift of the Provost and Fellows of King's College, Cambridge, who are the lay impropriators, and is held in conjunction with the adjoining parish of Bower Chalke, anciently called Burr or Burgh Chalke.

C. G. MOORE.

Broad Chalke Vicarage,
December, 1880.

The Registers

of

Broad Chalke, Wilts.

REGISTRUM DE JUNCTIS IN STABILI CONNUBIO A VICESIMO QUARTO MENSIS DECEMBRIS DIE IN A'NO D'NI 1562.

1562.

Bartholomew Penny & Sible Selby 24 Dec.
Peter ffletcher (?) & Elizabeth Witt 25 Dec.
Michaell Streete & Joane Jeffry 28 Jan.
Henry Good & Elizabeth Stayner 10 Feb.
John King & Mary Hunt 22 June
John ffanner & Alec Kendall 12 July
Roger Cashman (?) & Margaret King 15 Dec.

1563.

Robt Anthony & Joane Deyn 6 Sep.
John Bastard & Margerie Townsend 6 Oct.
Wm Scammell & Joane Hunt 9 Oct.
John Luke & Joane Penn 20 Oct.
John Chappell & Margerie Skinner 28 Nov.
Robert Golding & Agnes Odber 24 July
John Penny & Amy . . . . . 24 Jan.
Thomas King & Gyles Kendall 17 June
Ralphe Sweete & Marria Makerell 8 Nov.

1564.

John Gregorie & Alec White 12 April
Roger Strete & Margaret Ober 28 May
John Jeffery & Joane Savidge 31 Sep.
Stephen Strong 26 Oct.

1567.

Walter Perse & Julian King 7 Sep.
John Hardie & Agnes Whitmarsh 5 Oct.

1568.

Wm Odborne & Joane Burges 21 July
Thomas Fripp & Joane King 26 Sep.
Johne Cook & Joane Winter 27 Oct.
Thomas Taubet & Christian Dent 10 Nov.

1569.

Pet. New & Jone Cook 18 June
John West & Agnes Gerret 7 Oct.
Stephe' Due & Elizabeth Sydna 8 Oct.
Robt. Antrame & Jone Ogborne 12 Nov.
Tho. Strete & Jone Cook 16 Nov.
Tho. Dollman & Marie Line 6 Jan.

1570.

Alex. Kendall 7 June
John Hutchens & Dorothie Lodge 11 Nov.

1572.

Barthol. Good & Jone Odber 28 Nov.
Tho. Selwood & Edith Kendall 5 Dec.
John Willobye & Michaell Smith 17 Dec.

1573.

John Lawse & Jane Selwood 17 Jan.
Stephen Odber & Margaret Blake 2 April
Nicholas King & Olive Orchard 7 June
George Tayler & Mary Due 10 Sep.

1574.

John fforde & Jone Brine 22 June
Walter ffolyat & Alec Selby 8 Nov.
Barth. King & Jone Hunt 25 Nov.

1575.

John Brine & Jone Claidon 20 Feb.

Ralph Elmes & Alec Chotne 31 July
Morrice Loder & Elizabeth Townsend 14
    Aug.
Robt. Vassall & Jone Odber 28 Sep.
John King & Edith Chater 14 Nov.

1576.

John Newman & Jone Selwood 19 July
Richard Harford & Maud Addames 13 Sep.

1577, 1578, and 1579.

Wm Angod & Mary Baker 4 Nov.

1580.

Thomas Thripp & Elizabeth Symmes 1 May
Thomas Pike & Dorothy Penny 25 Sep.
Luke Stephens & Alec Warm . . . 16 Nov.
John Willins & Luce Everly 20 Nov.
Robt. Henston & Mary Temple 9 Jan.

1581.

Richard Stephens & Margaret Sainctlow,
    gent. 4 Sep.
Peter Bargoth & Jone Selby 18 Sep.
John Grey & Alec King 4 Oct.
John Plowman & Margaret Skinner 16 Oct.
John Pope & Alec Martin 23 Oct.
Ralph Symons & Annis Grater 29 Oct.

1582.

Henry Pennt & Margaret Strete 14 May
Richard Hunt & Margaret Savidge 28
    Nov.

1583.

Wm Gilbert & Mary Taylor 10 June
Edgar Thring & Mary King 23 June
Alex. King & Margaret King 9 Sep.
Thomas Okeford & Friseweed Langtre
    21 Oct.
Bartho. King & Agnes Selwood 13 Jan.
John Flower & Jone Miller 6 Feb.
John Small & Mary Savidge 17 Feb.

1584.

Thomas Cooke & Elizabeth Currgill 2 Nov.
Raphe Skinner & Mary Good 9 Nov.
Tho. Michell & Agnes Bryne 11 Nov.
Wm Brooke & Alec Brine 11 Jan.
Charles Jacob & Avice Penny 24 Jan.

1585.

John Lodge & Jone Whitmarsh 18 July
Richard Skeele & Judith Sherman 22 July
Wm Davis & Julyan Lantree 14 Nov.
Edward Human & Katherine fishe 12 Jan.
Walter Savidge & Julya Yellow 30 Jan.

1586.

John Penny & Michaell Streete 8 Aug.
John Earlye & Margaret Penny 10 Oct.
Christopher Hartford & Olive Stronge 30
    Oct.

1587.

Barthol. Penny & Agnes Norris 14 Aug.
John Marshman & Edith Kannor(?) 25 Oct.
Tho. Okeford & Dorothy Browne 30 Jan.

1588.

Walt. Wallis & . . . . Prestman 20 May
Nicholas Penny & Mary Kendall 30 June
John Lawse & Alec King 8 July
Edward Pitchland & Jane Aynold 22 July
Robt. Bostone & Margaret Browne 26 Sep.
Wm Gilbert & Alec Oliver 26 Oct.
Thomas Strong & Katherine Kendall 19
    Nov.

1589.

Henry Odber & Agnes Skinner 6 Oct.
Timo. . . . . & Ann Netton 3 Nov.
Henry Garland & Avice Laurence 22 Jan.
Wm Symmes & Dorothy Savidge 26 Jan.

1590.

Thomas Diarye (?) & Margaret felpes 27
    June
George Clitherly & Dorothy Streete 11
    Oct.

1591.

Roger Wagge & Alice Newman 21 June
Tho. finkly & Sibell Selwood 25 Oct.
John Pitchland & Elizabeth Plowman 6
    Dec.
John flower & Elizabeth Grout 14 Jan.

1592.

Edward Greene & Mary Scammell 9 July
Tho. Segrum & Elizabeth Loder 11 July
Nicholas Storky & Emaly Due 1 Aug.
Tho. Lambe & Jone Miller 7 Aug.
Henry faukner & Barbara Browne 8 Jan.
John Penny & Anne Sainctlow 29 Jan.
Michaell Angod & Anne Dowes 5 Feb.

1593.

Joseph Cooke & Edith Lushe 8 Oct.
Walter Edny & Julyan Savidge 11 Oct.
Richard Laurence & Joane Brine 24 Jan.

1594.

John Kendall & Mary Newman 27 May
Henry Good & Edith Lodge eod. die
John Oliver & Jone Golde 3 June
Stephen Odber & Jone Richarde 9 July

Michaell Ingram & Christian Bowne 28 Dec.

1595.

John Lodge & Marye Brine 17 Feb.
Henry Gilbert & Dorothie Wydall eod die
Thomas Windson & Julyan Davis 30 June
Christopher King & Luce Streete 7 July
John Ledford & Joane Symmes 29 Sep.
Nicholas Whitmarsh & Dennis North 6 Oct.

1596.

John Brocke & Jone Winterborne 30 May
Tho. Witt & Joue Cane 5 July
Wm Gilbert & Elizabeth Pitchland 10 Nov.
Tho. Lodge & Anne Cooke 21 Nov.

1597.

John Pillin & Margerie Miller 1 Feb.
Peter fletcher & Edith Rumsey 18 April
Georgius Bispon (?) et Maria Purches 4 July
Barthol. Dewe et Maria Thorne 10 Aug.
Robtus Cane et Agnes Elliott 25 Sep.
Barthol. Penny et Anna Savidge 21 Nov.
Johannes Hardye & Avicia Garland primo die

1598.

Arthurus Philpott et Elenora Golding 16 Jan.
Henricus Davis et Maria Skinner 24 Jan.
Johannes Kendall et Lucida King 26 June
Tho. Witt et Alicia Bartlett 3 July
Georgius Reade et Avicia Kendall 17 July
Guilielmus Antramme et Dorothea Kendall 24 July
Guilielmus Symmes et Agnes Moore 21 Aug.
Robtus Whitmarsh et Alicia Bower 2 Nov.

1599.

Johannes Targett et Marriana Bedford 25 April
Alexander Bell et Katherina Streete 25 June
Johannes Harte et Johanna Hardey 7 Sep.
John Griffine and Anne Good 19 Nov.
Thomas Witt and Johan New 26 Nov.

1600.

Raphe Streete & Joanne Kinge 14 Jan.
John Randole & Joan Savidge 14 Jan.
John Lunnam and Alice ffolliat 26 May
Thomas Lange and Elizabeth Lokesly 6 June
John folliote and Ann Randale 30 June

John Williams & Elizabeth Truncat 12 Oct.
John Morksom & Marie Payne 3 Nov.
John Lane & Joan Skilling 27 Nov.

1601.

John Lantry and Grace Thorne 20 April
Thomas Scammell & Elizabeth King 15 June
Will'm Lawes & Ann Randall 18 Jan.

1602.

Alexander Champion et Maria Angod 21 June
Thomas Holly and Alice Brine 2 Aug.
John Simmes and Joane Standy 14 Oct.
Robert Randoll and Alice Birkfeilde 28 Nov.

1603.

Walter Brine and Elizabeth Dawlinge 21 Feb.
John Miller and Mary Cooke 20 Aug.
James Witt & Mary Kinge 21 Aug.
Richard Shergoll and Annie Whitemarsh 7 Nov.

1604.

Anthony Birde and Elizabeth Hutchins 22 April
Ralfe White and Elizabeth Due 1 May
Daniell Deane and Katherine Lanctry same day
Thomas Witt and Anne Brine 4 June
John Sparke and ffortune Thomas 18 June
Walter Blake and Annie Kinge 8 Oct.
John Randoll and Tomisine Newam 4 Nov.
William Baberstooke and Sibell Eurtise 28 Jan.

1605.

William Savery and Annie Randoll 1 May
William Copall and Martha Browne 29 May
John Thringe and Mary Bennett 1 July
Walter Newman and Annie .... 7 Oct.
John Norris and Annie Odber 21 Dec.
John Combes and Anna Angod 3 Feb.

1606.

John Ploughman and Alice Witt 12 May
William Speiringe (?) and Jane Penny 9 Oct.
John Shergoll and Elizabeth Combs 23 Oct.
Robert Tillier and Katherin Bell 19 Jan.
Edward Goald and Marrian Streete 27 Jan.

Arthure Sloper and Dorithie Pitman 12 Feb.

1607.

John Randoll and Mary Thringe 27 April
Thomas Whitmarshe and Margery Angod 27 July
Robert Oake *alias* White and Jane Savidge 9 Nov.
Thomas Penny and Margeret Streete 26 Nov.

1608.

William Grey and Katherine Weekes 26 April
William Whitmarshe and Cisly Hutchins 4 July
Wilkes Shergoll and Avis Kinge 11 July
Walter Huyme and Elizabeth Randoll 25 July
John Randie and Dorchas Thomas same daye
Thomas New and Jane Streete 1 Aug.
George Tynte and Barbara ffaulkener 7 Dec.

1609.

Thomas Chater and Rachell Pillon 27 April
Christopher Silfe and Jane Randoll 25 Sep.
Robert Kinge and Martha Pillon 26 Oct.
Edward Simans & Mildred Kinge 22 Jan.

1610.

John Goldinge and Agnes Garrat 2 July
William White and Margery Bryne 14 Oct.
Thomas Kinge and Annie Phillpott 15 Oct.
Henry Norris and Joane Clenton 15 Oct.
Thomas Pitman and Judith Goode 28 Oct.
Silvester Pope and Annes Savidge 4 Nov.
Henry Lund and Margrett Streete 12 Nov.
Andrewe Deane and Elizabeth Pillen 81 Jan.

1611.

John Peny and Alec Angod 23 Jan.

1612.

William Michell and Avis Shergoll 11 May
John Eastman and Dorothy Kinge 7 June
Thomas Lambe and Mary Kinge 29 June
John Griffine and Avis Shergoll 8 July
Henry Gilbert and Denys Newman 24 Aug.
Will'm Gram'ell & Grace Kinge 25 Jan.
Clement White and Annie Savery same day

1613.

Edmund Sweetaple & Sibille Bennet 3 May
John Streete and Michaell Moxham 4 July
Leonard Weel (?) & widdow Tillier 18 Oct.
Henrie ffase and Hester Angod 24 Oct.
Thomas Dredge & Agnes Plowman 29 Nov.

1614.

John Amy and Jane Angod 30 May
Margery Wilkins & John Sheppard 28 June
Thomas Bennet & Margrett Sweetaple 13 Nov.
Epher Simmes & Grizill Hutchins 27 Nov.

1615.

Henry Hurst and Grace Angod 5 June

1616.

Cornelius Miles and Agnes Clinton 22 April
Thomas Antram and Edith Hibbard 10 July
Richard Lawes and Alice Lodge 15 July

1617.

Timothie Lodge & Anne Shergall 6 Oct.
Henry Penny & Edith Lodge 6 Oct.
Edmond White & Margaret Randall 12 Oct.
Walter Pilling & Alice Pinhorne 12 Nov.

1618.

Gabriell Kinge & Anne Whitmarsh 4 May
John Scot & Elizabeth Stoakes 26 July
Robert Whitmarsh & Alice Wyat 19 Oct.
John Meatyarde & Anne King 2 Nov.
Edward ffoxganger & Jane Cooke 23 Nov.
Thomas Kinge & Elizabeth Moxam 25 Jan.
John Saunders & Anne Whitmarsh 25 Jan.

1619.

John Not & Marie Barber 8 Nov.
Thomas Burton & Elizabeth Lodge 8 Jan.

1620.

John Hurrold & Grace Scammell 17 July
Henry Good & Elizabeth Penny 2 Oct.
Will'm Due & Jane Chalke 16 Oct.
Thomas Moxam & Michaell Penny 80 Oct.
Ralph Penn & Mary Moxam 29 Jan.

1621.

Edward Brine & Margaret Savidge 23 July
Edmond Coles & Dorothie Watkinson 14 Aug.
Edmond White & Marie Harris 20 Aug.

1622.

Wil. Bull & Edith Blacker 23 Sep.
(?) ander Francis & Joan (?) 7 Oct.
Anto. Angod & Eliz. Osburne Dec. 1
Joh. Bown & Elionor Phillips Jan. 8
Abraha. Penny & Mary ffalconer Feb. 11

1623.

Henry Sponge & Dorithee Sheargool June 6
Hen. King & Mary Randall Oct. 25

1624.

Henry Johnson & Jane Good Jan. 14.
Edward Henlot & Jane Randal Jan. 30
John Randall & Avies Berbry Feb. 12

1625.

John Bennett & Elizabeth Codimore July 4
Edward Osman & Grace Pennie Feb. 21

1626.

Henry Penny & Grace Kinge Nov. 6

1627.

M{ter} Walter Waller Vicar of Broad Chalk & Mrs Elizabeth Sainte Lowe d. of Mrs Elizabeth Sainte Lowe April 30
Richard Mullins & Marie Norrham 18 June
Rich. Best & Susan Street July 2
John More & Alice Lawes Aug. 5
Robert Bedford & Joan Dier Aug. 12
John Stocke & Marie Shergoll Feb. 7
Richard Barter & Hester Savage Feb. 25

1628.

Richard Skeel & Elizabeth Bill Aprill 22
Walter Whitmarsh & Anne Shergoll Aug. 21

1629.

Nicholas Sanders & Jane Good June 3

1630.

John Chubb & Jane Miles Jan. 29
John Lawes & Elizabeth Street May 31
Nicholas Welsted & Rachel Scammell July 29
John Marsheman & Catharin Frances Feb. 3

1631.

Christopher Sims & ffrancis Kinge 12 June

(?) Sa . . . nt & Marie Butler Oct. 19
Edmond Penny & Marie Lewsonne 26 Jan.

1632.

Thomas Penn & Elizabeth King June 4
Thomas Randall & Marie Randall 20 Aug.
Gulielmus Short & Maria Angod 25 Oct.
Stephanus Short & Elizabetha Randal 26 Nov.

1633.

Henricus Dandy (?) & Alecia Penn 29 April
Thomas Hixts & Elizabeth Grove Jan. 2
John Cobb & Dorothea Penny Jan. 14

1634.

Robert King & Frances Sims 19 July

1635.

Michal Farrant & Maria Garret 2 Aug.

1636.

Johanes Ford & Elizabetha Scammel 5 Oct.
George Bolton & Eleanora Bryne 29 Nov.
Johannes Feltham & Cecilia Rando 126 Jan.

1637.

Willm. Katky & Dorothie Folliat 8 May

1638.

Walter Bryne & Joane Frances April 26
William Penny & Ezth. Roberts 11 June
Thomas Penn & Mary Davies 21 Jan.

1639.

John Snooke & Margaret Street 5 May
William Harris & Ann Randol Sep. 30
Thomas White & Emma Simms Oct. 2

1640.

Willm. Pickford & Avis Brynie 20 April
John Holowayed & Elizabeth Ford 10 Aug.
William Deane & Margaret Shergal 12 Oct.

1641.

John Guier & Sisly Peanie May 4
Thomas Frances & Ann Jones May 14
John May & Jean Reed Aug. 9
John Lane & Avis Hueman (?) Nov. 1
William Segar & Edith Pride Nov. 27
Thomas Page & Jean Whitmarsh Jan. 17

1646.

Samuel Lisle of Breamore & Margaret Randoll of Broade Chalke March 30

1647.

Will. Good & Michael Mocksham May 4
Edward Chalke & Jeane Due July 26

1649.

William King & Margaret Street Oct. 16

REGISTRUM DE BAPTIZATIS AB INITIO MENSIS DECEMBRIS A'NO DM'I 1538 USQUE AD ANNUM 1579.

New written by Mr. HENRIE BROOKE: out of the Old Booke

1538.

Richard Deane s. John Deane 2 Dec.
John Townsend s. Wm Townsend 2 Dec.
Agnes Langtree d. Thos. Langtree 2 Mar.

1539.

Joanna Baron d. Wm Baron 13 April
Thomas Bryne s. Wm Bryne 25 April
Gyles Kendall d. Nicholas Kendall 25 May
Alec. Claydon d. John 30 May
Ralphe Heyre s. W^m 29 June
Joane Temple d. John 30 June
Wm Bryne s. Rob^{rt} 15 Aug.
John Collens s. Nicholas 17 Aug.
Bartholomew Newman s. W^m 30 Aug.
Alec. King d. John 6 Oct.
John Fanner spurius Johannis 3 Nov.
Avis Lyme d. John 5 Nov.
John Pyper s. John 6 Nov.
Wm Rouff s. Edward 26 Nov.
Alec. Good d. Alexander 11 Dec.
Agnes Yelow d. W^m 11 Dec.
Agnes Whitmarsh d. Walter 13 Dec.
Agnes Staple d. Stephen 8 Jan.
Elizabeth Hussey d. W^m 11 Jan.

1540.

Alexander Curtes s. Henry 30 March
Nicholas Kendall s. W^m 8 May
Avis Gawnt d. Roger 13 Aug.
Agnes Bayne d. Thomas 25 July
Joane Whitmarsh d. Roger 13 Aug.
Edward Langtree s. Thomas 23 Sept.
John Lawse s. John 30 Oct.
Sybell Pyper d. Robt. 19 Nov.
John Yelow Wm Yelow sons W^m 3 Jan.
Avis Kendall d. Nicholas 17 Jan.
Julyan . . . sons d. Leonard 25 Jan.
John Barnard s. John 20 March
Luce Butler d. Jacob 20 March
Owin King s. John 28 March

1541.

Ralphe Stronge s. John 30 April
Wm Webb s. John 9 June
Bartholomew Huszey s. W^m 17 June
Stephen Golden s. John 30 July
Alex. Good s. Alex. 11 Aug.
Elizabeth Brine d. Robt. 22 Aug.
Alec. Gregorie d. John 27 Aug.

Annis Heire d. W^m 31 Aug.
Alec. Willis d. Walter 6 Sep.
Edward King s. Tho. 2 Oct.
Margaret Bryne d. W^m 3 Oct.
Olive Rendall d. W^m 10 Oct.
Joan Whitmarsh d. Roger 31 Oct.
Joan Deane d. Jo. 9 Nov.
John Temple d. John 17 Dec.
John Clever s. George 15 Jan.
Wm Gay s. W^m 9 Feb.
Katherine Pix (?) d. John 10 Feb.
Joan Dean d. W^m 5 March
Katherine ffishe d. of Tho. 6 March

1542.

Joan Lyne d. Jo. 5 April
Alec. Selwood d. Tho. 8 April
Katherine ffanner d. Jo. 22 April
Sybill Selby d. John 26 April
Joan Wisedome d. St. 26 May
Joan Qurtis d. Henrie 29 July
Henricus Rendall s. Nicholas 2 Aug.
Henricus Laurence s. W^m 18 Aug.
Henricus Huszey s. W^m 23 Aug.
Joan Gool d. John 23 Sep.
Wm Bryne s. Tho. 1 Oct.
Elizabeth Wisedome d. Steph. 10 Oct.
Wm King s. Tho. 17 Oct.
Agnes Selwood d. Tho. 18 Oct.
Ralphe White s. Joh. 22 Oct.
Alex. Ayre s. W^m 30 Oct.

1543.

George Chlyver s. George 1 Jan.
Marks Bryne s. Tho. 3 Jan.
Agnes Deane d. W^m 5 Jan.
Elizabeth Steving d. W^m 9 Jan.
Aves Bryne d. Robt. 10 Jan.
Thomas Line s. Tho. 7 Feb.
John Willis s. Walter 7 Feb.

1544.

Tho. Temple s. of John 4 April
Margaret Selby d. John 15 April
John Rendall s. Thomas 16 April
Alec. Bryne d. W^m 23 April
Wm Vanner s. John 6 May
Sybly Collens d. W^m 8 June
Stephen Laurence s. Alex. 1 Oct.
Wm Rendall s. Nicholas 3 Oct.
Tho. Wisedome s. Stephen 16 Oct.

Walter Gregorie s. John 11 March
Avis Temple d. Jo. 22 Aug.*

1548.

Helene Bryne d. John 18 May
Marie Rendall d. Tho. 17 May
Julyan Townsend d. W^m 20 May
John Due s. John 23 May
John Kentchinton s. W^m 3 June
Ralphe Curtes s. Henrie 5 July
John Bryne s. Robt. 7 Aug.
Thomas Lantree s. John 17 Aug.
Henrie Bryne, Alce Brine 8 Sep.
Mary King d. Tho. 9 Sep.
Alce King d. John 29 Sep.
Joan Wisedome d. Stephen 12 Jan.
Wm Amis s. W^m 17 Jan.
Joan Due d. John 2 Sep.

1550.

Tho. Rendall s. Nicholas 6 Jan.
Alce Savidg d. W^m 15 Jan.
Amy Lantree d. Tho. 23 Jan.
John Townsend s. W^m 1 March
Elizabeth Ames 12 March
John Peny s. W^m 27 March

1551.

Dorothy Newman 25 May
Margaret Ames 2 July
Elizabeth Bryne 6 Sep.
Tho. Rendall 10 Sep.
Ames Butcher 20 Sep.
Christian Savidge 19 Sep.
Alce King 21 Oct.
Joan Rendall 22 Oct.
Olive Strong 24 Oct.
John Deane 29 Oct.
Dorothy Wisedom 8 Dec.
Philip Kentchenton 22 Jan.
Thomas Witte 24 Jan.
Edith Penny 30 Jan.
Hugh King 18 Feb.
Alce Rendall 23 Feb.
Thomas Townsend 26 Feb.

1552.

Joane Whitmarsh d. Roger 20 Sep.
Joane Cooke d. John 24 Sep.
Wm Shergall s. Tho. 9 Oct.
Dorothy Logge d. John 10 Nov.

* In the original Register this entry occurs at the bottom of the page, and on the top of the following one the date 1548 is written in the margin. There is no entry in the original MS. between the years 1544 and 1548.

Joane King d. Tho. 20 Nov.
Mary Deane d. W^m 20 Aug.

1553.

Thomas King s. Tho. 2 Jan.
Dorothy Temple d. John 9 Feb.
Joane Witt d. Tho. 12 Feb.
John Clarke s. W^m 12 March
Julyan Bryne d. Robt. 20 April
Julyan Rendall d. Henry 2 May
Richard Alyn 27 Sep.

1554.

Tho. Lodge 28 Sep.
Joane Lawden 29 Sep.
John Dean, Barth. Deane 29 Sep.
Nicholas Deane 15 Jan.
John Doning 25 Feb.
Isabell Selbie 1 March
Stephen Collens 4 March
John ffann s. John 30 March
Joane fish 30 May

1555.

John Rendall s. John 26 Sep.
John Street s. Michaell 30 Sep.
John Netton s. Davy 15 Oct.
Stephen fish s. Thomas 20 Jan.

1556.

Wm Savidg s. W^m 3 Feb.
Thomas Gowles s. John 15 Feb.
Margaret King d. Gabriell 3 March
Marie King d. Thomas 22 March
Thomas Odberr s. Richard 25 March
John Lodge s. John 2 April
Margaret Cook d. John 4 June
Joan King d. John 9 July
Edmond Smith s. Tho. 29 Sep.
Ellen Wisedome d. Step. 20 Oct.
Joane Skinner d. W^m 12 Dec.
John Sillige 18 Nov.
Margerie Staple 13 Nov.
Henrie Netton s. David 29 Nov.
John Due s. John 29 Nov.
John Street s. Thomas 29 Nov.
Elizabeth Due d. John 17 Feb.
Henry Holland 10 Feb.
Amy Bryne d. W^m 3 Feb.
Margaret Streete d. Nicholas 1 March

1557.

Alce Odber d. Richard 14 April
Margaret Rendall d. Tho. 11 June
Thomas Skinner s. John 30 June
Mary Angod d. Thomas 15 July
Thomas Cook s. John 14 Aug.

Joane Shergall d. Tho. 4 Sep.
Ellen Townsend d. Tho. 16 Oct.

1558.
Tho. Rendall s. Alex. 21 March
John Bryne s. W^m 25 March
Owen Savidg s. W^m 28 March
John Streete s. Tho. 23 April
Joane King d. Gabriell 23 May
Mary Skinner d. John 30 May
John Deane s. W^m 23 June
Timothy Lodge s. John 24 June
Henry Symmes s. John 27 July
John Lowe s. John 18 Aug.
Sybell Rendall d. Henry 25 Aug.
Avis Peny d. W^m 26 Sep.
Alce Curtes d. Henrie 10 Dec.
Amy Smith d. Mr Tho. 12 Dec.
Wm Odber 20 Dec.
Adrey King d. John 20 Jan.
Blase Shergall s. Tho. 3 Feb.
Nicholas Skinner s. W^m 9 Feb.
Symon ffish s. Tho. 12 Feb.

1560.
Henrie ffinckly s. W^m 6 Nov.
Michaell Netton d. John 15 Dec.
Wm Nurry s. W^m 20 Feb.
Margaret Savidge d. W^m 30 Feb. (*sic.*)
Thomas Shergall 30 Feb.
Michaell Antrame d. Tho. 8 March

1561.
Ellen Townsend d. Nicholas 6 April
Henrie Rendall s. Henrie 8 April
Joane Streete d. Alex. 13 April
Joane Penny d. W^m 13 April
Wm Hinke s. Richard 12 Oct.
Edith ffanner d. John 20 Jan.
Mary Good d. John 6 March
Thomasin Hogget d. Tho. 7 March
Sibell Netton d. John 27 May

1562.
John Rendall s. Alex. 4 May
John Bastard s. John 6 May
Alce Townsend d. W^m 8 May
Tho. Lodge s. John 15 April
Agnes Skinner 12 July
Thomas Due 29 July
Thomas Scammell s. W^m 16 Aug.
Robt. ffishe 29 Aug.
Alce King d. Gabriell 29 Aug.
Mathew finckly d. (*sic*) W^m 20 Sep.
Dorothy Evens d. Richard 20 Sep.
Alce Simmes d. John 23 Sep.

Mary Sawman d. Tho. 26 Sep.
John Golden s. Robt. 18 Oct.
Agnes Good d. Henrie 21 Dec.
Stephen Cook s. John 16 Jan.
Sybell Thomas d. John 16 Jan.
Mary Wallis d. Henry 2 Feb.
John Wallis s. Henry 2 Feb.
Isabell Streete d. Tho. 18 Feb.

1563.
Mary Rendall d. Alex. 21 Feb.
John Townsend s. Nicholas 1 March
Julian Lantree d. Tho. 25 March
Mary Bedford d. John 21 April
Joane Miller d. Henry 25 April
Joane Woodlocke d. W^m 10 May
Roger King 20 May
Alce Antramme 20 May
Alce Nurry 28 July
Agnes Almesdeed d. Richard
John Penny
Henry Aynes s. Tho. 18 Oct.
Alexander Rendall s. Henry 6 Dec.
Margaret Penny d. Barth. 11 Feb.

1564.
Sybell King d. John 5 May
Maude Whitmarsh d. Tho. 5 May
Walter Due s. John 16 June
Isabel Woodlocke d. W^m 24 June
Joane King d. Tho. 5 July
Grace King d. Edward 2 Aug.
John King s. Gabriell 5 Aug.
Joane Penny d. John 5 Aug.
Henry Good s. Henry 28 Sep.
Tho. finckly s. W^m 1 Nov.
Tho. Savidg s. W^m 12 Nov.
Margaret Shargall d. Tho. 12 Nov.
Joane frestone d. John 1 Jan.
Alce King d. John 1 Jan.
Thomas Thomas s. John 12 Jan.
John Bedford s. John 25 Jan.

1565.
Isabell Townsend d. Nicholas 23 June
Joane King d. Richard 7 July
Mary King d. Tho. junior 5 Aug.
Mary Skammell d. W^m 5 Aug.
Amy Netton d. John 31 Aug.
Isabell Woodlocke d. Robt. 24 Sep.
Tho. Whitmarsh s. Tho. 5 Nov.
Robrt. Strete s. John 9 Nov.
Edith Lodge d. John 15 Dec.
Tho. Smith s. Richard clerici 3 Jan.
Wm King s. Edward 15 Feb.
Nicholas Penny s. W^m 27 Feb.

1566.

Joane Golden 23 April
Michaell Strete d. Ralph 6 Aug.
Joane Olyver d. John 12 Sep.
Avis Penny d. Barth. 27 Sep.
Michaell Angod s. Tho. 21 Oct.
Marke Wallis s. Henry 26 Nov.
Robt. Bedford s. John 7 Dec.
Nicholas Whitmarsh s. Tho. 26 Dec.
Katherine King d. Edward 27 Dec.
Bartholomew Penny s. W^m 14 March
Alce freston d. John 14 March

1567.

Edith Brine d. Tho. 16 April
Alce Hardye d. John 23 June
Peter Blewet 2 July
Joane King d. Tho. 9 July

1568.

Christian Perse d. Walter 17 July
Richard Locke s. John 4 Aug.
Dorothy Streete d. John 12 Sep.
Wm Ogborne s. W^m 10 Dec.
W^m a bastard 26 Dec.
John Scammell s. W^m 30 Dec.
Joane Gregorie d. John 13 Feb.
Thomas Antramme s. Tho. 27 Feb.
Stephen Good s. Henry 27 Feb.

1569.

Ann Savidg d. W^m 24 April
Mary Nurry d. Richard 12 June
Agnes Gerret d. W^m 17 July
Alce Penny d. Barth. 28 Aug.
Elner Golden d. Robt 15 Sep.

1571.

Margerie Gregorie 22 July
Ralph Strete 31 July
Henry Curtes s. Alex. 5 Aug.
Agnes King 15 Aug.
Jone Rendall d. Alex. 23 Aug.
Joane Nurry d. Richard 8 Oct.
Amy Whitmarsh d. Walter 17 Nov.
Margaret Streete d. Tho. 20 Nov.
Ann Rendall d. Alex. 7 Dec.
Henry Penny s. W^m 12 Dec.

1572.

Joyce Frestone d. John 2 Jan.
Walter Bryne s. Tho. 11 Feb.
Christobell Penny d. John 4 April
George Gerret s. John 14 April
Nicholas Hardye s. John 1 May
Juell Savidge s. W^m sen. 24 May
Joane Good d. Barth. 14 June
Joyce King d. Edward 12 Oct.

1573.

ffortune Gregorie 20 March
Nicholas ffrancis s. John 22 March
George Lawse s. John 12 April
Ralph Due s. Tho. 1 July
John Strete s. John 1 July
John Penny s. W^m jun^r 22 Sep.

1574.

Dionize Parkins d. Robt 31 Jan.
Richard Bedford s. John 22 Feb.
Henry Odber s. Stephen 6 March
Alexander Good s. Henrie 24 March
Amy Good d. Barth. 27 March
Agnes Selwood d. Tho. 4 April
Elizabeth Whitmarsh d. Tho. 18 April
Jane Curtes d. Alex. 15 June
Agnes Nurry d. Richard 16 June
Wm Penny s. Barth. 7 Sep.
John Strete s. Ralph 18 Oct.
Jane Hardy d. John 7 Nov.
Joane New d. Peter 19 Dec.

1575.

Marie King d. Tho. 2 Jan.
Agnes Rendall d. John 23 Jan.
Wm Lawse s. John 12 April
Mary King d. Barth. 12 April
Katherine Streete d. Tho. 25 June
Sibbell Witt d. Nichomead 8 July
Wm Penny s. John 8 July
Alce Taylor d. John 3 Aug.
Joane Ward d. Richard 28 Aug.
Agnes Odber d. Stephen 18 Sep.
Tho. Bryne s. John 30 Oct.
Elizabeth Good d. Barth. 6 Nov.
Stephen Netton s. Ralphe 20 Nov.

1576.

Elner Cable d. Robt 20 Jan.
Richard Due s. Steph. 20 Jan.
Wm Angod s. W^m spur. 7 March
Alce ffrancis 14 June
Alce Witt d. W^m 12 Aug.
Walter Newman s. John 2 Sep.
Wm Scammell s. W^m 9 Sep.
John ffolyat s. Walter 14 Oct.
Mary Curtes d. Alex. 1 Nov.
Avis Bryne d. John 1 Nov.
Maude Penny d. of W^m 11 Nov.
Joane Due d. of Tho. 14 Nov.
Jane Rendall d. of Henry 25 Nov.
Agnes Good d. of Henry 24 Dec.

1577.

Julyan Baker filia M^{ri} Baker Clerici 24 March
Mary King d. of Nicholas 14 April

Sible Lawse d. John 25 May
Tho. Street s. John 2 June
Alex. Penny s. Barth. 14 June
Edward Barter s. Tho. 7 July
John Rendall & Alex. sonnes of John 14 Aug.
Sible Bennet d. Edward 24 Aug.
Robt. Pick 7 Sep.
Margaret Slite d. John 6 Oct.
Luce Streete d. Ralphe 13 Oct.
Tho. Angod s. W^m 24 Nov.
Robt. Elmes s. Ralphe 8 Dec.
Annis Whitmarsh d. Tho. 20 March

1578.

Wm King s. Tho. 18 April
Edith Due d. Tho. 13 May
John Elmes s. Ralphe 15 May
Stephen Savidge s. John 16 May
Mary King 19 May
Ralphe Miles s. Ellize 3 June
Grace King 10 June

1579.

Wm Angod s. W^m 10 May
Tymothy francis s. John 23 May
Mary Humby 24 May
Ralphe Good s. Henry 24 May
Henry Good s. Barth. 24 May
Dionize North d. Richard 28 May
John Rendall s. Tho. 7 June
Elizabeth Curtes 21 June
Margaret Rendall 24 June
Henry Witt 12 July
John Lawse s. John 2 Aug.
Joane Wyat d. W^m 2 Aug.
Wm Selwood s. Tho. 9 Aug.
John Plowman s. John 9 Sep.
Christian ffolyat d. Walter 21 Sep.
Elizabeth Angod 25 Sep.

1580.

Thomas Penny s. W^m 27 March
Margaret Elmes d. Ralph 10 April
Edward Nicholas 24 Aug.
Charitas Penny d. Barth. 3 Oct.
Dorcas & Thomas s. & d. W^m 11 Oct.
John Davis s. W^m 21 Oct.
John Newman 10 Nov.
James Witt s. Tho. 26 Nov.

1581.

Wm Rendall s. Henry 5 Jan.
Mary Good d. Barth. . . . . .
Robt. Henston 10 Feb.
Phillip Humby 19 March
Walter Angod s. Tho. 25 March
John Winterborne s. Tho. 15 April

Annis Rendall d. John 24 April
Melford King s. of Barth. 30 May
Henry Lawse s. John June 2
Annis Savidge d. of W^m 20 Aug.
Margaret Davis d. of W^m 6 Oct.
Martha Pillin d. of John 22 Oct.
John Thripp 26 Nov.
John Grey s. John 26 Dec.

1582.

Mary Angod d. W^m 25 Jan.
Mary Bennet 6 Feb.
Marrian Strete d. Thomas 23 Feb.
Annis Curtes 3 March
Walter ffolyat 29 March
Annis Savidge d. John 2 April
Richard Humby s. of Phillip 30 May
John Sherman 8 Aug.
Michaell Due 22 Sep.
Thomas Plowman 23 Sep.
Jane Penny 26 Sep.
Alce Everet spur. Henry 20 Oct.
Mary Cook d. Stephen 15 Nov.
John Gray s. John 26 Dec.
Robt. Henston s. Robt. 27 Dec.
Annis Good d. Barth. 6 Jan.
Henry Rendall s. Henry 15 Jan.
Wm Cook s. John 21 Jan.
Mathew Humby spurius 21 Jan.
John Penny s. Barth. 27 Jan.
Stephen Angod s. Tho. 7 Feb.
ffortune Hunt d. Richard 21 Feb.
Edith Ellet d. Humfrey 24 Feb.
Jane Good d. Henry 3 March

1583.

Anne Due d. Tho. 13 April
Richard Wilkins s. Pet. 26 May
Mary Penruddock d. John Esquire borne
    ye 20 of June 7 July
Sara Stephens d. Richard gent. (borne y^e
    10 July) 14 July
Sybell ffrancis 1 Sep.
John Humby s. Phillip 15 Sep.
Henry Gilbert s. W^m 21 Oct.
Dorothy Rendall d. Nicholas 3 Nov.
Jane Rendall d. John 9 Nov.
Elizabeth Pillin d. John 13 Dec.
Thomas Lawse s. John 15 Dec.
Alex. Cook s. John 26 Dec.
Joane King d. Alex. 10 Jan.
John Bennet s. Edward 12 Jan.
John Thring s. Edgar 31 Jan.
Valentine Rendall s. Tho. 6 Feb.
Dorothy King d. Barth. 15 Feb.

1584.

Joane Savidge d. W^m 12 April

Anne King d. Barth. 9 May
John Thomas s. W^m 20 May
Dorothy Hunt d. Richard 2 Aug.
John Loxlye s. Tho. 11 Aug.
Clement Bryne s. John 16 Aug.
Nicholas Stenton (?) s. Ralph 30 Sep.
Grace Penny d. W^m 12 Oct.
Mary Prow d. Tho. gent. 18 Oct.

1585.

Thomas Odber s. Tho. 25 Jan.
Annes Curtes d. Alce 25 April
Alce Brooke d. W^m 20 May
Dionize s. John Newman 6 June
John Good s. Henry 15 Aug.
Agnes Skinner d. Ralph 22 Aug.
John folyat s. Walter 4 Sep.
Priscilla Pillin d. John 26 Sep.
Richard Angod s. Tho. 20 Oct.
Edward Rendall s. Alex. 7 Nov.
Andrew Deane s. Tho. 21 Nov.
Stephen Davis s. W^m 26 Dec.
Edward Thring s. Edgar 9 Jan.
Agnes Plowman d. John 17 Jan.
Agnes Savidge spur. d. Walter 5 Feb.
Katherine Nicholas d. Richard gent. 21 Feb.
Tho. King s. Barth. 5 March

1586.

Grace Savidge 7th d. Steph. 31 March
Walter Bennett s. Edward 17 April
Amy Streete d. Richard 1 May
Wm Grudd s. W^m 29 May
Wm Due spur. s. John 24 June
Tho. Davis s. W^m 14 Aug.
Anthony Angod s. W^m 17 Aug.
Joseph Cook s. John 18 Sep.
John Rendall s. John 25 Nov.
John Flower s. John 25 Dec.
Ralphe Penne s. Henry 28 Dec.

1587.

Sara Loxly d. Tho. 14 April
Michaell Selwood d. * Tho. 14 April
Christobell Savidge d. W^m 1 May
Ralph Penny s. John 15 May
Avis King d. Tho. 17 June
Henry Erley s. John 6 Aug.
Rachell Pillin d. John 8 Sep.
Harbart Nicholas s. Richard 10 Sep.
ffrancis King & Grace s. & d. of Tho. 24 Oct.
Avis Lodge d. John 27 Jan.
John Cook s. John 28 Jan.
Anthony Selby s. Tho. 30 Jan.
Step. Streete s. Richard 30 Jan.

* Sic.

1588.

Wm Skinner s. Ralph 31 March
Henry Rendall s. John 24 June
Gabriell King s. Barth. 24 Nov.
Annis Savidge d. Walt. 2 Feb.
Judith Good d. Henrie 12 Feb.
Henrie Good s. John 28 Feb.
Jane Angod d. W^m 2 March
Mary Bryne d. John 16 March

1589.

John Savidg s. Steph. 28 March
Ann Loxly d. Tho. 1 April
Walter Pillin s. John 27 April
Henry Selwood s. Tho. 1 May
Wm Marshman s. John 30 May
Maude Savidge d. W^m 15 June
Wm Penny s. Nicholas 4 July
Briget Flower d. John 23 Sep.
Joane Bostone d. Robt 8 Oct.
Thomas Elmes s. Ralphe 1 Nov.
ffrancis Streete s. Rich. 16 Nov.
Joane Pook d. ...... 19 Nov.
John Early s. John 7 Dec.
Avis Hunt d. Richard 27 Jan.
Thomas Cook s. John 28 Jan.
Alce Lodge d. John 7 Feb.
Elizabeth Penny d. Pet. 8 March
John Penny s. John 20 March
Thomas King s. Tho. 22 March

1590.

John Skinner s. Ralphe 29 March
Margaret Sainctlow d. John gent. 13 May
Jane Follyat d. Walt. 16 May
Thomas King s. Nicholas 25 Sep.
Henry Plowman s. John 29 Sep.
Jane Clinton d. Ralphe 29 Sep.
Richard Dyer s. Tho. 14 Oct.
Tymothie Lodge s. Timoth. 4 Nov.
Jane Bennet d. Edward 4 Nov.
Briget Pillin d. John 1 Jan.
Ralphe Elmes s. Ralphe 14 Feb.
Alce Angod d. W^m 14 March
Mary Bostone d. Robt 16 March

1591.

Christopher Simmes s. W^m 27 March
Alce Marshman d. John 3 April
Barthol. King s. Barth. 16 April
Katherine Loxly d. Tho. 18 April
Anne Pitchland d. Edward 30 April
Anna Sainctlow d. John gent. 30 May
Elizabeth Angod d. Tho. 29 June
Elizabeth Penne d. Henry 15 Aug.
Mary Francis d. John 15 Sep.
Annis Odber d. Henry 15 Oct.
Annis Thring d. Edgar 10 Nov.

Margaret Cook d. John 27 Nov.
Christopher Plowman s. John 29 Nov.
John Dyer s. Tho. 25 Dec.
Phillip Steele s. Richard 2 Jan.
John Shergall s. Tho. 5 March

1592.

Katherine Penny d. Nicholas 1 April
John Rendall s. Alex. 25 April
Katherine Penny d. Pet. 29 May
. . . . . . Tho. 31 Maii
Alce Pitchland 10 June
Marie Cook 11 June
Richard Savidge 16 Sep.
Nicholas Savidge } s^s W^m 17 Sep.
Wm Savidge
Bartholomew Segar 17 Sep.
Elizabeth Penny d. John 4 Feb.
Thomas Finkly s. Tho. 10 Feb.
Mary Savidge d. Steph. 3 March

1593.

Thomas Simmes s. W^m 29 March
James Hunt s. Richard 29 June
Alex. ffollyat s. Walt. 19 July
Henry Odber s. Henrie 19 Aug.
Henry Loxly s. Tho. 2 Sep.
Martha Sainctlow d. John gent. 25 Nov.
Joane Savidge d. Owin 30 Dec.
Brightweed Clenton s. Ralphe 30 Dec.
John Lamb s. Thomas 3 Feb.
Mary Wivall d. Tho. 20 Feb.
Thomas King s. Nicholas 3 March

1594.

Amy Angod d. Michaell 6 May
John Segar s. Tho. 13 May
Thomas Dyer s. Tho. 16 May
Elizabeth Penny d. John 8 June
Mary Penny d. Peter 12 June
John Stocky s. Nicholas 23 June
. Annis Olyver d. John 5 July
Solomon & Margaret Penny s. & d. Bartho.
    28 July
Mary Cook d. Joseph 22 Sept.
Thomas Penne s. Henry 12 Oct.
John Cook s. John 25 Oct.
Nicholas Rendall s. John 31 Oct.
Christopher Cook 14 Feb.

1595.

Gryzell Hutchens d. John 2 March
Dina King d. John 2 March
Amy Angod d. Tho. 30 March
Thomas Bryne s. Walt. 30 March
Steph. Edney s. Walt. 10 May
Elizabeth King d. Tho. 14 May
Dennis ffrancis s. John 20 May

Elizabeth Sainctlow d. of John, gent. 7
    June
John King s. Barthol. 17 June
Edward Bryne s. Tho. 2 Oct.
Joane Penny d. Nicholas 4 Oct.
John Odber s. of Henry 5 Oct.

1596.

Elizabeth Lodge d. John 10 Jan.
Margaret Savidg d. W^m 14 Jan.
Robt Bedford s. John 18 Jan.
Thomas Penny s. John 16 Feb.
Edward spurius s. Katherine King 3
    March
Michaell Penny d. Pet. 28 March
Amy Angod d. Michaell 25 April
Joane Lamb d. Tho. 25 April
Margaret Wyvall d. Tho. 25 July
Amy King d. Thomas 10 Aug.
Margaret Edney d. Walt. 8 Oct.
Ralph ffrancis s. John 16 Oct.
Ralphe Segar s. Thos. 10 Nov.
Thomas Hunt s. Richard 17 Nov.

1597.

Edward King s. Christopher 23 Jan.
Stephen Cook s. John 11 Feb.
Mary Dier d. Thomas 3 March
John Rendall s. John 25 March
Tho. Gilbert s. Gulielmi 2 July
Henricus Good s. Henrici 10 July
Petrus Skeele s. Richardi 10 July
Johannes Sainctlow s. Johannis 14 Aug.
Stephan . . . s. Thomæ 7 Sep.
Thomas Lodge s. Thomæ 20 Sep.
Anna Angod d. Tho. 9 Oct.
Alex. King s. Bartholomei 29 Nov.
Rowland Savidge s. Steph. 18 Dec.
Stephanus Clynton s. Rodolph Dec.

1598.

Thomas francis s. Joannis 2 Feb.
Jacobus (?) & Jane Cook s. & d. Johannis
    18 Feb.
Guilielmus Odber s. Henrici 17 March
Editha Lodge d. Joannis 18 March
Johannes Cane d. Robti 18 April
Guilielmus Scammell s. Guilielmi 11 Aug.
Abrahamus Penny s. Johannis 10 Sep.
Gertruda Sainctlow d. Joannis gener. 18 Oct.

1599.

Johannes Chater s. Thomæ 28 Jan.
Thomas Dewe s. Bartholomei 8 Feb.
Alicia Penne d. Henrici 8 March
Henricus Davye s. Henrici 9 March
Charitas Bryne d. Thomæ 13 March
Thomas Newman s. Alexandri 23 March
Dorothea Shargall d. Thomæ 27 March

Robertus Fishe s. Joannis 27 March
Maria Pennie d. Joannis 1 April
Thomas Lamb s. Thomæ 13 May
Hester Savidg & Juliana Savidg daughs.
    Guilielmi 13 May
Alexander Rendall s. Johannis 25 May
Anthonius Wilkins s. Johannis 27 May
Joanna Dyer d. Thomæ 28 June
Elizbetha Whitmarsh d. Thomæ 29 June
Thomas Cook s. Johannis 15 July
Joanna Edney d. Walteri 20 July
ffardinando Sayntlo s. Johannis Sayntlo 9
    Sep.
Anna ffrancis d. Alexandri ffrancis 30 Nov.
Nicholas Penny s. Bartholomew Penny 21
    Dec.

1600.

Christabell . . . d. John . . . 14 Jan.
Alexander Randole s. John 23 Feb.
John Griffin (?) s. John 23 Feb.
John Steel s. . . . Steel 19 March
Avis Penny d. Nicholas Penny 13 April
    [Four or five entries here are undeci-
    pherable from the effects of damp.]
Jean Good d. Harry Good 27 July
John Witt s. Thomas Witt 31 Aug.
ffrancis Whitmarsh d. Henry Whitmarsh 1
    Oct.
William Joye s. William 14 Dec.
Robert Cane s. Robert Cane 14 Dec.
Thomas Fish s. John Fish 19 Dec.

1601.

Thomas ffrances s. Alice ffrances 30 Jan.
Johan Davie d. Henrie Davie 30 Jan.
. . . Sentlowe d. John Sentlow 2 Feb.
Henrie Penny s. John 2 Feb.
John ffaukner s. Henry 8 Feb.
Henrie Randale s. John 8 Feb.
Katheren ffrances d. John ffrances 13
    Feb.
Grace Cook d. John 18 Feb.
Henry Penny s. Peter 10 March
Marie Gerret d. An 2 May
Lanclot Bell s. Alexander 7 June
John Smale & Elizabeth Smale children
    of William 24 June
Alexander Streete s. Thomas 9 Aug.
Walter Whitmarsh s. Nicholas 20 Sep.
Katherine Wilkins d. John 16 Dec.

1602.

Priscilla Hart d. John 1 Jan.
Avis Griffine d. John 16 Jan.
John Scammell s. George 23 Jan.
Rebecka King d. Katherine spur. 13 Feb.

Darathie Coal d. Edwarde 24 Feb.
Mary Shergale d. Thomas 28 Feb.
Mary ffrancis d. Alexander 26 March
Mary Joye d. William 28 March
Thomas Grove s. William 25 April
Edgar Randall s. Alexander 16 May
Joan Cooke d. Mary Cooke 25 May
Johannes ffolliate s. Johannis ffoliate 23
    June
Dorithy Wayefolde d. Dorythy Wayefolde
    28 June
Charles Angod s. Thomas Angod 21 Sep.
Mary Savidge d. William Savidge 14 Oct.
Elizabeth Edny d. Gualter Edny 20 Oct.
John Penny s. John Penny 21 Oct.
Thomas Witt s. Thomas Witt 1 Nov.
Annis Whitemarsh d. William White-
    marshe 6 Nov.
Mary Angod d. of Thomas Angod 26
    Nov.
Jane Randoll d. Thomas Randoll 3 Dec.

1603.

John Harby s. John Harby 13 March
William Dew s. Bartholomew Dew 13
    March
Jane Lamme d. Thomas Lamme 20 March
Anna Penny d. Nicholas Penny 3 April
John Randoll s. Robert Randoll 7 May
Katherine Penruddocke d. Mr Thomas
    Penruddocke 16 June
Jane Odber d. Henry Odber 25 June
Joye Smale d. William Smale 2 July
Robert Holly s. Thomas Holly 10 July
William Randol s. John Randol the farmer
    of Moulsell* 9 Sep.
Elizabeth Bell d. Alexander Bell 20 Oct.
Alexander Lawes s. William Lawes 10
    Dec.
Michaell Penny d. John Penny of Radishe
    farmer† 20 Jan.
Anna Miles d. Ralphe Miles 25 Jan.
Ann Griffine d. John Griffine 29 Jan.
Rachell Scammell d. George Scammell 25
    Feb.
Walter ffolliate s. John ffolliate 27 Feb.
Alice Witt d. Jeames Witt 7 March
Sara Streete d. Ralfe Streete 7 March

1604.

Alice ffrannces d. Alice ffrannces 8 May
Daniel Thringe s. Edgar Thringe 27
    May

---

* Properly Mount Sorrel, now called Mouse-
hole.
† Now Reddish House.

Alexander Miller s. John Miller 28 May
Ellinor Goale d. Edward Goale of Stoake
     Verden 13 July
Joane Holly d. Thomas Holly 21 Sep.
Idy Angod d. Thomas Angod 23 Sep.
Lawrence Sayntlow s. Mʳ John Sayntlow
     30 Sep.
George Penruddocke s. Sir Thomas Pen-
     ruddocke 30 Oct.
Avis Randoll d. Thomas Randoll 31 Oct.
Alice Harte d. John Harte 18 Nov.
William Whitemarshe s. Nicholas White-
     marsh 25 Nov.
Elinor Brine d. Walter Brine 21 Dec.
Mary Deane d. Daniell Deane 21 Dec.
Elizabeth ffrances d. Alexander ffrances
     2 Jan.
Ralfe Streete s. Thomas Streete 27 Jan.
Ellinor Penny d. Bartholomew Penny the
     younger of Stoake Verden 27 Feb.
Emme Whitemarshe d. Thomas White-
     marshe 20 Feb.
John Browne base s. Martha Browne 20
     Feb.
Idy ffishe d. John ffishe 3 March

1605.

Annis Randoll d. Alexander Randoll *alias*
     Newman 5 May
Thomas Angod s. Thomas Angod 29
     May
Robert Randoll s. Robert Randoll 16
     June
William Collens s. John Collins 20 July
Jane Shergoll d. Thomas Shergoll of
     Hirkgam 21 July
Sible Savery d. William Savery 11 Aug.
Henry Penny s. John Penny of Stoake
     Verden 18 Aug.
Anthony Smale s. William Smale 18 Aug.
Grace Edme d. Walter Edme of Stoake
     Verden 24 Aug.
Avis Phripp d. John Phripp 4 Sep.
Rachell Hardie d. John Hardy of Stoake
     Verden 4 Oct.
Edward Witt s. Thomas Witt 26 Oct.
Mary Davy d. Henrie Davy 28 Oct.
William Baberstoke s. William Baber-
     stoke 8 Nov.
Robert Scammell s. George Scammell 22
     Dec.
Joane Streate base d. Marrian Streate 26
     Dec.
Jane Miles d. Ralfe Miles 5 Jan.
John Randoll s. John Randoll of Moul-
     sell the elder 10 Jan.

Robert Norris s. John Norris 19 Jan.
Richard Evans s. John Evans 19 Jan.

1606.

Jane Lawes d. John Lawes 25 March
Elizabeth Sayntelow d. Mʳ John Saint-
     low 26 May
Katherine Streete d. Ralphe Streete 27
     July
Edmond Deane s. Daniell Deane 2
     Aug.
Thomas Odber s. Henry Odber 3 Aug.
William Penruddocke s. Sir Thomas Pen-
     ruddocke 9 Aug.
Elizabeth Randoll d. Thomas Randoll 25
     Oct.
Thomas Holly s. Thomas Holly 29
     Oct.
Jane Due d. Bartholomew Due 10 Dec.
Elizabeth ffolliat d. John ffolliat 11 Dec.
Huyge Randoll s. John Randoll of Stoake
     18 Jan.
Mary Witt d. Thomas Witt the younger
     1 Feb.
John Street s. John Street 6 March
Thomas Phripp s. John Phripp 4 March

1607.

Grace Kinge d. William Kinge 28 March
Tomisin Pillen base d. Rachell Pillen 10
     April
John Cane s. Robert Cane 26 April
Avis Speeringe d. William Speeringe 21
     June
George Lawes s. John Lawes the younger
     24 July
Mary Thringe d. John Thringe 29 July
Alice Lawes d. William Lawes 5 Aug.
William Deane s. Daniell Deane 4 Sep.
John Wilkins s. John Wilkins 23 Sep.
William Penny s. John Penny of Stoake
     Verden 27 Sep.
Elizabeth Scammell d. George Scammell
     18 Oct.
Ann Randoll d. Robert Randoll 31
     Dec.
Millesant ffrances d. Alexander ffrances
     17 Jan.
Melior Baberstocke d. William Baber-
     stocke 29 Jan.
Joane Miles d. Ralfe Miles 30 Jan.
Mary Collens d. John Collens 14 Feb.
Edmund Penny s. Bartholomey Penny of
     Stoake the younger 1 March
Avis Newman d. Walter Newman 28
     March

1608.

Thomas Witt s. James Witt 28 March
Idie Phripp d. John Phripp 17 April
John Randoll s. Alexander Randoll *alias* Newman 16 July
Annis Penny d. Thomas Penny 31 Aug.
Robert Whitmarsh s. Nicholas Whitmarsh 24 Sep.
Joane Shergoll d. Thomas Shergoll 8 Oct.
Walter Oake *alias* White 18 Dec.
Annis Griffen d. John Griffen 25 Jan.
Elizabeth Witt d. Thomas Witt the elder 3 March
Annis Randoll d. Thomas Randoll the younger 8 March
Henry & William Pennyrott sons William Pennyrott 29 March

1609.

Mary Miller d. John Miller 26 March
John Randeie s. John Randeie of Knighton 7 May
John Speiringe s. William Speiringe 9 Aug.
Ann Shergoll d. Wilks Shergoll 25 Aug.
Walter Holly s. Thomas Holly 18 Sep.
Dorathy ffolleat d. John ffolleat 24 Sep.
Ralfe Streate s. Ralfe Streate 18 Oct.
Dorathy Whitmarshe d. William Whitmarshe 22 Oct.
Richard Scammell s. George Scammell 15 Nov.
Jane Streate d. John Streate 26 Feb.
Thomas Deane s. Daniell Deane 9 March

1610.

Barbara Collens d. John Collens 6 May
Edward Penny s. Johannis of Stoke 10 June
Jane Thringe d. John Thringe 6 July
John Kinge s. Robt Kinge 8 July
Margret Myles d. Ralfe Myles 19 Aug.
Nathaniell Lawse 21 Sep.
Margrett Shergoll d. Richard Shergoll 30 Sep.
Alexander Rendoll s. Robert Rendoll 5 Oct.
John Witt s. Thomas Witt 11 Nov.
John Miller s. John Miller 13 Jan.
Joane Rendoll d. John Rendoll 13 Jan.
Moses Newman 25 Jan.
John Lawes 10 Feb.
Henry Shergoll s. Weeke Shergoll 17 Feb.
Henry Griffine 17 Feb.
Christopher Rendoll 20 Feb.

1611.

Martha Owen d. Peter Owen Cleri 12 May

John Peny s. Bartholomew Peny of Stoke 12 June
Dorothye Deane d. Daniell Deane 4 Sep.
Ralph Witt 29 Sep.
Avis Rendoll d. Alexander Rendoll 2 Oct.
Cicely Rendoll d. Thomas Rendoll 13 Oct.
Dominicke bastard of Alce Wyat 14 Feb.
Anne Streete d. Ralph Streete 15 Feb.
Alexander ffrancis 15 March
Jane Eilffe d. Christopher Eilffe 19 March

1612.

Jane Griffine 29 March
Michaell & Mary Penny dd. John Peny the younger 30 March
Jane Whitmarshe 30 May
Syble Deane d. Andrew Deane 32 *(sic)* May
Thomas Rendoll s. Thomas Rendoll 8 June
Thomas Priest s. Edward Priest 27 June
Mary King d. Thomas Kinge 26 July
William Peny s. Thomas Peny 16 Aug.
Christopher Scammell s. George Scammell 23 Aug.
Walter Gilbert s. Henry Gilbert 18 Oct.
Walter Newman s. John Newman 11 Nov.
John Dewe s. Bartholomew Dewe 11 Dec.
Cornelius Miles s. Rafe Miles 14 Feb.
Margrett Peny d. John Peny 21 Feb.

1613.

Anne Thring d. John Thring 3 April
Elizabeth Holly d. Thomas Holly 4 July
Jane Lawes d. John 11 July
Julian White d. Clement 11 July
Elizabeth Speering d. W^m 18 July
John Peny s. John 28 July
Als Witt d. Thomas 15 Aug.
Margret Jones d. Willm 22 Aug.
Toby Randall s. Robt 12 Sep.
Jane ffolliatt d. John 18 Sep.
Perteisty (?) Witt d. James 24 Sep.
Thomas s. Andrew Deane 17 Oct.
Anne d. Samuell Whitehead 2 Feb.
Cornelius s. Thomas Witt 13 Feb.

1614.

Michaell d. Alexander Randall 22 June
Josias s. John Blake 24 June
Michaell d. Thomas Lambe 11 Sep.
William s. William Smale 2 Oct.
Tymothy & Anthony ss. William Jey 21 Oct.
Elizabeth d. John Streete 26 Nov.
Elizabeth d. Edward Priest 21 Dec.
Joane d. Wm Michell 23 Dec.

Mary d. Edward Scammell 1 March

1615.

William s. Willm. Lawes 23 April
Henrie s. Walter Newman 18 May
Andrew s. Andrew Deane 4 June
Mary d. Thomas Randall 11 June
William s. Robert King 18 July
Amy d. John Veltam 30 July
Gabriell s. Thomas King 17 Sep.
Elizabeth d. Christopher Yelfes 24 Sep.
Sibille d. John Thring 25 Nov.
Thomas s. Henrie Gilbert *alias* Stud 18 Oct.
. . . . . s. Ralph Miles 10 Dec.
Thomas s. Alexander ffrancis 17 Dec.
Jane d. Thomas Holly 10 Jan.
Christopher Peny s. Thomas 28 Jan.
Thomas s. John Randall 27 Feb.

1616.

Thomas s. John Peny 13 April
Joane d. Thomas Randall 14 April
Mary d. Robert Randall 21 May
John s. John Lawes 16 Dec.
Nicholas s. Robert King 22 Jan.
William s. Thomas Holly 9 Feb.
John s. Nicholas Whitmarsh 12 Feb.

1617.

Luce d. Alexander Randall 5 April
Willm s. Bartholomew Segar 29 June
Solomon s. Thomas King 31 Aug.
Jane d. John ffoliat 21 Sep.
Andrew s. Edward Priest 5 Oct.
Charles s. Walter Newman 14 Dec.
Emme d. Christopher Simmes 1 Feb.
Thomas s. John Thringe 4 Feb.
John s. Mr William Jones, gent., 22 Feb.
Henry & Willm ss. John Penny 25 Feb.
Antgre (?) d. John Blake 20 March

1618.

Willm s. Willm Angod 4 April
John s. James Witte 12 April
Thomas s. Mr Adam Waters, Clark, 26 July
Thomas s. Andrew Deane 2 Aug.
Anne d. George Scammell 28 Sep.
William s. William Speering 17 Nov.
Timothy s. Thomas King 25 Jan.
Edward s. Thomas Penny 9 Feb.
John s. Gabriell King 28 Feb.
Henrye & Marie s. & d. Henry Scud *alias* Gilbert 13 March
Elizabeth d. John Randoll of Knighton 17 March

1619.

Anne d. John Scot 3 April
Taberet d. Christopher Yellowes 18 July
William s. Edward ffoxhanger 24 Oct.
Ellis s. Edward Priest 26 Dec.
Willm s. Henry Norris 27 Feb.

1620.

Michaell d. John Penny the younger 15 April
Elizabeth d. John Saunders 19 April
Dorothie d. Thomas Randoll 19 May
Thomas s. Mr Adam Waters, Clark, 28 May
Thomas s. Timothie Lodge 11 June
Elizabeth d. Bartholomew Penny of Stoake 25 June
Anis d. Willm Michell 3 Sep.
Christopher s. Thomas Holland 19 Nov.
Elizabeth d. John Thringe 18 Dec.
Gabriell s. Gabriell King 21 Jan.
Mary d. John Not 11 Feb.
Anne d. Mr William Grove junior 12 March
Sarah d. Christopher Simes 18 March

1621.

Mary d. Timothy Lodge 2 April
James s. Edward ffoxanger 15 April
Anne d. William Speering 9 June
Mary d. John Randoll 16 June
Thomas s. Thomas King 5 Aug.
John s. Ralph Pen 7 Oct.
Thomas s. George Scammell 23 Nov.
Thomas s. Peter Steven (?) 9 Dec.
Henry s. John Penny 16 Jan.
John s. Henry Scud *alias* Gilbert 30 Jan.
Thomas s. Willm Angod 24 March

1622.

John s. Willm Due 31 March
Alce spur. d. Elinor Lylly 10 April
Willm s. Edward Brine 8 May
Charles s. John Saunders 12 May
Henry s. Henry Good 26 May
Joane d. Andrew Deane 29 June
John Notte s. John 30 June
Robert Rushe s. Robert Rushe 6 Oct.
Sarah Yelf d. Christopher Yelf 18 Dec.
John s. John Paradise 24 Jan.
Allice d. Henry Studd 9 Feb.

1623.

Elizabeth d. Mr Will. Grove 30 March
Bartholomew Seger s. Bartholomew 17 June
Elenor Dew d. William 9 Aug.
Alice Francis d. Alexander 15 Sep.

Anna Lodge d. Timothie 16 Sep.
Anne Shergoll d. Robert 18 Sep.
Margaret Skeel d. Peter 2 Oct.
Elizabeth Angood d. Anthonie 19 Oct.
Francis Erneley d. Edward 14 Dec.
Christobell Spering d. William 15 Dec.
William King s. Gabriel 31 Dec.
Anne Lodge d. Timothie 16 Sep.
Gartrude Good d. Henrie 16 Jan.
William Michel s. William 20 Jan.
Margaret Scammell d. George 4 Feb.
Alexander Pennie s. John 19 Feb.

1624.

Henrie Sims s. Christoph. Sims 11 April
Edward Byfelchom s. Christopher Byfelchom 11 May
Henrie Pen s. Ralph Pen 3 June
Willem King s. Thomas King 22 July
Honor Fox d. Edward Fox 15 Aug.
Mari Penni d. Abram Penni 28 Nov.
Michaell d. Anthony Angod 5 Dec.
Michaell d. Thomas Moxam 12 Dec.
Edward s. Walter Rennell 21 Dec.
Henry s. Willeam Angod 28 Dec.
Abraham s. Christopher Goold 9 Jan.
Alexander s. Ralfe Streat 15 Jan.
Henry s. Henry Lawes 31 Jan.
John s. Willem Skenner 20 Feb.
Alse d. Thomas Gilford 24 Feb.

1625.

Dennes d. Edward Brine 8 April
Mary d. Thomas Yellow
Edward s. John Sanders 15 May
Willem s. Willem Grove 19 May
Alexander Frances s. Alexander Frances 2 Oct.
Thomas s. Thomas Burden 4 Dec.
Timothi Lodge s. Timothi Lodge 18 Dec.
Nicholas s. John Not 18 Dec.
Jane Deane d. Audry Dean 27 Dec.
John Savidge s. Nicholas Savidge 1 Jan.
Ralph Good s. Henry Good 8 Jan.
Jafra Whit s. Edward Whit 29 Jan.
Elizabeth Peni d. John Penney 5 March

1626.

Edith Norris d. Henry 2 April
Margaret Rendoll d. John 7 May
Alice Lawes d. Henry 8 May
Ane Penny d. Bartholomew Penny 6 June
Willum Gilburd s. Hinry Gilbord 16 July
Elezabeth & Barbry Penney dd..Abram Penney 11 Sep.
Christibell d. Gabrell King 15 Oct.
Thomas s. Thomas Gillbord 26 Nov.

Elzebeth Whit d. John Whit 21 Dec.
Robert s. Thomas King of Stoke Verden 21 Dec.
Thomas s. Walter Bennet 7 Jan.
John Nay s. Richard Nay 20 Jan.

1627.

Agnis Stoeks d. William Stoeks 3 May
William Cook s. Christopher 6 May
Michael Pennie d. Henrie Pennie 26 May
William Angood s. Antone Angood 3 June
Jane Fox d. Edward Fox 15 July
Henrie Priest s. Edw. Priest 6 Aug.
Christopher Simmes s. Christopher 24 Aug.
Elizabeth Mullins d. Richard Mullins 10 Nov.
Richard Randol s. Thomas Randol 24 Feb.
John Sanders s. John Sanders 9 March
Alice Lodge d. Timothie Lodge 10 March
John Penie s. Abraham Penie 12 March
John Lawes s. Henrie Lawes 20 March

1628.

John Good s. Henrie Good 2 April
Rachel Randol d. Thomas Randol 2 April
Nicolas Francis s. Alexander Francis 5 April
Jane Heylock d. Robert 14 April
John Bedford s. Robert Bedford 4 May
Walter Penny s. John Peny 8 Aug.
Margaret Orvington d. Thomas Orvington 16 Aug.
Marie White d. Edmund White 7 Sep.
Elizabeth Moxam d. Thomas Moxam 21 Sep.
Elizabeth Barter d. Richard Barter 21 Feb.
Joane Savage d. Nicholas Savadge 14 Feb.
William Savadge s. William Savadge 25 Feb.
William King s. Gabriell King 10 March
John Randoll s. Will'm Randoll 15 March

1629.

Henry Norris s. Henry Norris 12 April
Susan Archer d. William Archer 25 April
Jeane Dewe d. William Dewe 25 April
Walter Bennet s. Walter Bennet 10 May
Mary d. Henry Good 17 May
Elizabeth d. Anthonie Angood 28 June
Margaret Brine d. Edward Brine 25 Aug.
Joyce Penny d. Henrie Penny 13 Sep.
Ann Whitmarsh d. Walter Whitmarsh 27 Sep.
Walter Savage s. John Savage 29 Nov.
Amie Skeele d. Richard Skeele 17 Jan.
Jane Gilbert d. Thomas Gilbert 31 Jan.
Maria Sims d. Ch. Sims 13 Feb.

Elizabeth Deane d. Andrewe Deane 20 Feb.

Tho. Lodge s. Timothie Lodge 28 Feb.

Edward & Marie Foxe s. & d. Edward Foxehanger 28 Feb.

1630.

Ellen Lillie d. John Lillie 11 April

Anne Good d. Hen. Good the younger 14 April

John Saintloe s. John Saintloe of London Marchant 21 June

Will'm Frances s. Alex. Frances 25 July

Hen. Dowe s. Hen. 29 Aug.

Thomas Orvington s. Tho. 1 Nov.

Jeane Molins d. Richard Molins 14 Nov.

Nickolas bastard s. Joane Lambe 14 Nov.

Jane Nott d. John Nott 2 Jan.

Avis Whitmarsh d. Walter Whitmarsh 23 Jan.

Will'm Dew s. Will'm Dew 18 Feb.

John White s. John White 16 Feb.

Christian d. John Chubb 27 Feb.

John Martchman s. John Martchman 18 March

1631.

John Randal s. John Randal 5 June

Eliz. Brine d. Edward Brine 24 July

Will'm Archer s. Will'm Archer 17 Aug.

Mary Molins d. Richard Molins 20 Nov.

Samuel King s. Gabriel King 30 Nov.

Marie Moxom d. Th. Moxom 4 Dec.

John   s. Hen.   4 Dec.

Richard Wag. s. Richard Wag 11 Dec.

Ann Fox d. Edward Fox 11 Dec.

Marie Sanders d. John Sanders 1 Jan.

Alice Penny d. Ralph Penny 9 Feb.

1632.

John Savage s. John 25 March

Ann Spratt filia peregrinantis Richard Spratt 27 March

. . . . Savadge d. Nicholas Savadge 29 April

Ann Lawes d. Alexander Lawes 21 May

William Lodge s. Tymothy Lodge 10 June

Henry Penny s. Henry Penny 24 June

Anthony Penny s. John Penny 1 July

William Grove s. Thomas Grove 1 Aug.

Charles King s. John 2 Sep.

Avis Angod d. Anthony Angod 2 Sep.

Robert Haylock s. Robert Haylock 19 Oct.

Ann Short d. William Short 16 Dec.

Thomas Randal s. Thomas Randall 27 Dec.

Dorothy Skeele d. Richard Skeele 6 Jan.

William Marshman s. John Marshman 9 Jan.

. . . . Oventon d. Thomas Oventon 13 Jan.

Avis Whitmarsh d. Walter Whitmarsh 23 Jan.

Alice Evens 27 Feb.

Ann Archer 10 March

Elizabeth Myles 17 March

Susan Bryne 17 March

1633.

Elizabeth Good d. Henry Good 10 June

Thomas filius peregrinantis 17 Nov.

Bartholomew Penny s. John Penny 21 Nov.

Joanna Savage d. John Savage 15 Dec.

John Chubb s. John Chubb 12 Jan.

Elizabeth Davis d. Henry Davis 9 Feb.

1634.

John Francis s. Alexander Francis 25 April

Angod Evens d. Thomas Evens 30 April

William Savidge s. William Savidge 4 May

Martha Foxhanger d. Edward Foxhanger 13 May

Phillip White s. John White 8 June

John Smyth s. John Smyth 23 July

Anthonie Angod s. Anthonie Angod 31 Aug.

Ann King d. Gabriel King 28 Sep.

Phillip Hexts s. Thomas Hexts 5 Oct.

John Lawes s. John Lawes 12 Oct.

Joan Cook d. Christopher Cook 26 Oct.

Ann Molins d. Richard Molins 2 Nov.

Anthonie Lodg s. Timothie Lodg 2 Dec.

Elizabeth Randol d. Thomas Randol 14 Dec.

Simon Penny s. John Penny 15 Jan.

William Lawes s. Alexander Lawes 2 Feb.

John Short s. William Short 8 Feb.

Sarah Penny d. Ralphe Penny 22 Feb.

1635.

Edward Bryne s. Edward Bryne 30 March

John Penny s. John Penny 5 April

Ann Penny d. Nicholas Penny 5 April

Thomas Moxam s. Thomas Moxam 19 April

Ann Symmonds d. Elizabeth Symmonds 19 Aug.

Bartholomew Ovington s. Thomas Ovington 26 Aug.

Ann Penny d. Abraham Penny 13 Sep.

Walter Whitmarsh s. Walter Whitmarsh

Henry White s. Edmond White 14 Feb.

Christopher Smith s. John Smith 25 Feb.

Mary Streat d. John Streat 28 Feb.

Anne Sanders d. John Sanders 13 March
Walter Wagg s. Richard Wagg 20 March

1636.

John Archer s. Anthony Archer 19 April
John Randol s. Henry Randol 11 May
Mary Lawes d. John Lawes 15 May
Mary Faranton d. Michael Farenton 22 May
Elizabeth Savadge d. Nickolas Savadg 19 June
William Good s. Henry Good 26 June
John Bennet s. Walter Bennet 3 July
Isack Savadge s. William Savadge 4 Sep.
William Foxe s. Edward Foxe 11 Sep.
Christopher Ford s. John Ford 9 Oct.
Thomas Feltam s. John Feltam 30 Oct.
Bartholomew Penny s. John Penny 6 Nov.
Laurence Saintloe s. Mr Laurence Sayntloe 2 Feb.
Joane Penny d. Abraham Penny 20 Feb.
Joane Penny d. John Penny 19 March

1637.

George Lawes s. George Lawes 10 April
George Bolton s. George Bolton 16 April
Anthony Lydford s. Robert Lydford 1 May
Avis Odbur d. Th. Odbur 9 June
Elizabeth Randol d. Hen. Randol 18 June
John Good s. Henry Good 9 July
Frances Chub s. John Chub 9 July
Elizabeth Cook d. William Cook 17 Sep.
Ambrose White s. Edmond White 29 Sep.
.... Dewe s. Thomas Dewe 8 Oct.
Anne Bennet d. Walter Bennet 3 Nov.
Abraham White s. John White 3 Dec.
.... Short d. William Short 24 Dec.
.... d. John .... 30 Dec.
.... Ovington s. Thomas Ovington 29 Jan.

1638.

Joane d. Richard Molins 15 July
Sarah d. Abraham Penny 22 Aug.
John Ford s. John Ford 14 Oct.
Mical Penny d. Ralph Penny 21 Dec.
William Andrewes s. William Andrewes 1 Jan.
William Odbur s. Thomas Odbur 3 Feb.
Martha Archer d. Anthony Archer 15 Feb.
William Smith s. John Smith 17 Feb.
John Lawes s. John Lawes 28 Feb.

1639.

John Randol s. Henry Randol 23 May
Tho. Holly s. Tho. Holly 23 June

Joane Goldin d. John Golding 4 Aug.
Marie Penny d. Charles Penny 11 Aug.
Elizabeth Penny d. John Penny 11 Aug.
Edward Foxe s. Edward Foxe 6 Oct.
Hen. King s. Gabriel King 27 Oct.
Laurence Penny s. Mr Abraham Penny 25 Dec.
John Witt s. John Witt 26 Jan.
Joane Savage d. William Savadg 9 Feb.
Thomas Penn s. Th. Penn 16 Feb.
Edith Ledford d. Rob. Ledford 16 Feb.
John Farrant s. Michael Farrant 15 March
Roger White s. Edward White 15 March

1640.

Laurence Saintlo s. Laurence Saintlo gent. 4 April
Ann Randol d. Hen. Randol 26 April
Alice Bolton d. George Bolton 10 May
Ralph s. John Smith 25 June
John Randol s. John Randol 5 July
Elizabeth Randol d. Thomas Randol 2 Aug.
Whytmarshe bastard son of John Whytmarshe & Ann Woodford 6 Sep.
Elisabeth Odburre d. Thomas Odbur 6 Sep.
Avis Whitmarsh d. Walter Whitmarshe 4 Oct.
Mary Due d. Thomas Due 8 Nov.
Margaret White d. Thomas White 15 Nov.
William Odburre s. William Odburre 12 Jan.
John Golden s. John Golden 12 Jan.
Charitie Wagg d. Rich. Wagg 30 Jan.
Jeane Folliat d. John Foliat 12 March

1641.

Debora Penny d. Mr Abraham Penny 25 March
Bridget natural d. F. Frances 24 April
Margaret Deane 25 May
Henrie Holly 13 June
John Odburre 25 July
Cornelius Short 22 Aug.
John May s. John May 10 Oct.
John Randol s. John Randol 14 Nov.
Charles Whitmarshe s. Walter Whitmarshe 17 March
Thomas Andrewes s. Will. Andrewes 4 Feb.
Ann Archer d. Anthony Archer 3 March
Will. Lawes s. John Lawes 3 March
Elenor Ferant d. Michael Ferant 20 March

1642.

Ann Lawes d. John Lawes 27 March
Charles Savadge s. Will. Savadge 1 April

Frances Saintlowe d. Mr Laurence Saint-
lowe 6 April
Joyce Randol d. Tho. Randol 26 June
Michel Penny d. Ralph Penny 3 July
Phillip Bennet s. Walter Bennet 26 Aug.
Elizabeth Odburre d. William Odburre 4
Sep.
James Witt s. John Witt 18 Sep.
John Guyer s. John Guyer 6 Nov.
Ann Seagar d. William Seagar 13 Nov.
Mary Randol d. Henry Randol 1 Jan.
Mary Bolton d. George Bolton 8 Feb.
William Aubrey s. Mr Richard Aubrey
borne on 2 March bap. 13 March
John Hudson s. John Hudson 15 March
Mary Holly d. Thomas Holly 19 March

1643.

John Saintloe s. Mr Laurence Saintloe bap.
25 March, borne 21 March 1642.
Marie Deane d. William Deane 23 April
Elizabeth Dewe d. Thomas Dewe 21 May
Jane Randole d. John Randole 11 June
Edith Penny d. Henry Penny 12 July
Rose Randole d. John Randole 28 July
Elizabeth Francis d. Thomas 15 Oct.
Marie Scammel d. John Scammel 19 Nov.
Laurence Smith s. John Smith 3 Dec.
John Randole s. John Randole 5 Dec.
John Penny s. Charles Penny 19 Dec.
Thomas Chubbe s. John Chubbe 23 Dec.
Thomas Golding s. John Golding 14 Jan.
Richard Moulins s. Richard 18 Feb.
John White s. Thomas White 28 Feb.
John Folliott s. John Folliott 10 March
William Segor s. William Segor 24 March

1644.

Cornelius Witte s. Cornelius Witte 14 April
William May s. John May 28 April
John Holly s. William Holly 1 May
Elizabeth Phrippe d. John Phrippe 7 July
Henry Miles s. Isaac Miles 28 July
Thomas Dewe s. Thomas 6 Oct.
Anne Odburre d. William Odburre 20 Oct.
Anne Lawes d. William Lawes 20 Oct.
Elizabeth Savage d. William Savage 8
Dec.
Susane Andrew d. William Andrew 13
Dec.
Sarah Segor d. Bartholomew 22 Dec.
Thomas Ledford s. Robert Ledford 12 Jan.
Anne Randole d. John Randole 15 Jan.
Elizabeth Saint Loe d. Laurence Saint Loe,
gent. 25 Feb.
Andrew Gwire s. John Gwire 25 Feb.
Katherine Streete d. John Streete 26 Feb.

1645.

Marie Randole d. Thomas Randole 13
April
John s. John Bundy 23 April
Joane d. William Whitemarsh 8 May
Jasper s. Micaell Huntly 15 June
Marke s. John Randole 2 Sep.
*Thomas Aubrey s. of Richard Aubrey,
gent. & of Deborah his wife was borne
2 Sep. & was bap. 10 Sep.
Thomas Witte s. Cornelius Witt 24 Sep.
Bartholomew s. William Segor 22 Nov.
William s. William Pennie 30 Nov.
William s. William Deane 22 Dec.
Jane d. Thomas Dewe 28 Nov.
Nicholas s. Bartholomew Segor 26 Jan.
Jane d. Henry Randoll 1 March
George s. Thomas Reade 3 March
Henry s. Charles Pennie 5 March
Anne Saint Loe d. Laurence St. Loe 7
March

1646.

Jane d. John Odburre 8 April
Jane d. John Bundy 18 May
Thomas s. Thomas White 5 July
George s. John Scammell 2 Aug.
Thomas s. John Lawes 9 Aug.
Phillip s. Cornelius Witt 7 Oct.
Mihill d. Robert Ledford 29 Nov.
Dennis d. Walter Whitmarsh 1 Dec.
John s. William Odberr 3 Dec.
Walter Foliat s. John ffoliat 9 Dec.

1647.

Ralphe Miles s. Isaac 12 April
William Lyle s. Samuel 13 April
John Chub s. John 7 May
Rebeccka King
Joane Holly
Jeane Penny
Laurence Saintloe s. Laurence 1 Jan.
Ann Whitmarsh d. William 19 Oct.
Hester Deane d. Thomas 10 Nov.
Ann Randoll d. . . . . . 16 Dec.
Elizabeth Baker d. Christopher 6 Feb.
Nicholaus Savage s. William 3 March
Robert Witt s. John Witt 10 March

1648.

Abigaile Sloper d. John Sloper, Vicar, 4 May
John Lodge s. John Lodge 9 May
Thomas Randol s. John Randol 19 May
Henry White s. Henry 8 June
Jone Randolph d. Henry Randolph 9 June

* A pencil note says, "the autograph of John
Aubrey" (signed) E. Awdry.

Thomas Read s. Thomas 14 June
Deborah Penny d. Charles Penny 7 Sep.
Ann Miles d. Cornelius 21 Sep.
John Deane s. William 13 Jan.
Ann Good d. Hen. Junior of Moulesan 19
Jan.
Robert White s. Jefery 5 Feb.
Thomas Deane s. Thom. 16 March
Edward Chalke s. Edward 17 March
Mary Bundy d. John *borne* 11 Nov.

1649.

John Streete s. Ralph 10 April
Joyce Orchard d. Richard 10 April
Randolph Lodge s. Timothie 28 May
Henry Randol s. Henry 13 June
Elizabeth Sims d. John 26 Aug.
Martha Newman d. Charles 2 Sep.
Philippa King d. John 7 Sep.
Avis White d. Henry 25 Oct.
Timothy Lodge s. John 13 Nov.
Thomas Read s. Thomas 15 Nov.
Joyce Bond d. Edward 19 Nov.
Richard King s. Robert 21 Nov.
Henry Lawes s. John 23 Dec.
Mary Randol d. Alexander 1 Jan.
Daniel White s. Thomas 25 Jan.
John Sloper s. John 7 Feb.
Anthony Archer s. Anthony 19 Feb.
Henry ffoliot s. John 24 Feb.
Denis Segar d. Will. 4 March

1650.

fflorence Saintloe d. Laurence 2 June
William Holly s. Will. 21 May
Elizabeth Harris d. Timothy 23 May
William Whitmarsh s. Will. 11 June
John Goulding s. John 16 June
Elizabeth Good d. Henry 22 June
Joyce Penny d. John 30 June
Thomas Randoll s. Tho. 5 Aug.
Elizabeth Whitmarsh d. Walter 9 Aug.
William King s. Will. 18 Aug.
John Orchard s. Richard 15 Sep.
Michaell Good d. Will. 13 Oct.
John Pen s. Henry 20 Oct.
Walter Segar s. Barth. 10 Nov.
Rebecca Witte d. Cornelius 8 Dec.
Alice Huntly d. Michaell 29 Dec.
William Chalke s. Edward 9 Feb.
Mary White d. Jeffery 9 Feb.
Joyce Odber d. Will. 26 Feb.

1651.

Edward Baker s. Christo. 31 **March**
John Bundy s. John 8 May
Lucy Angood d. Henry 13 May

Thomas Wit s. John 19 **May**
Tho. Scammell s. John 11 June
William Penny s. Charles 14 July
Anne Penny d. John 17 Aug.
Mary White d. Hen. 18 Aug.
Mary Harding (?) d. John 3 Sep.
Elizabeth Dew d. Tho. 19 Sep.
John Lodge s. Timothy 2 Oct.
Ann Lodge d. John 10 Oct.
Lucy Randoll d. Alexander 12 Nov.
Margaret Archer d. Antho. 27 Nov.
Joan Deane d. Tho. 4 Dec.
Martha Bennet d. Walter 8 Dec.
Thomas Segar s. William 10 Dec.
William Grove s. William 11 Dec.
Mary Miles d. Cornel. 11 Dec.
Nicholas Slop (?) s. John 22 Jan.
Jane Streate d. Ralph 2 Feb.
John Penny s. John 11 March
John Lisle s. Samuell 16 March

1652.

John Chalke s. Edward 9 April
Robert Ledford s. Robert 28 April
Richard Shergoll s. Richard 19 May
Henry Good s. Henry 23 June
Henry Norris s. Hen. 23 June
William Randoll s. John 13 July
Jane Harris d. Timothy 8 Aug.
Timothy Wag s. Timothy 11 Aug.
Ann Read d. Tho. 2 Oct.
Ann Wit d. Corne. 25 Oct.
Joane Randoll d. Tho. 8 Nov.
John King s. John 20 Dec.
Tho. White s. Jeffery 1 Jan.
John King s. William 18 Jan.
Annis Holly d. William 29 Jan.
Anne White d. Hen. 2 Feb.
Edward ffolliat s. John 2 Feb.
Jane White d. Tho. 15 Feb.
Elizabeth Penny d. Christo. 19 Feb.
Michaell Lawes d. John 27 Feb.

1653.

Thomas Lodge s. John 25 April
Hester Whitmarsh d. William 18 May
Jone Randoll d. Henry 1 June
Mary Bennet d. Tho. 30 July
Daniell Deane s. William 15 Aug.
Samuell Archer s. Antho. 7 Sep.
Nicholas Wit s. John 8 Sep.
Elizabeth Slop (?) d. John 20 Sep.
Thomas Mell (?) s. Leonard 13 Oct.
*Walter Harris s. John 5 July

* (Sic), this should have bin entered hyher.

A REGISTER OF THE BIRTHS OF CHILDREN AFTER THE 29TH DAY OF SEPTEMBER MADE IN THE YEARE OF OUR LORD 1653 ACCORDING TO THE ACT.

1653.

Elizabeth Grove d. William gener. born 30 Sep.
Lydia Bundy d. John 17 Dec.
Katherin Witt d. Cornelius 26 Dec.
Mary Pen d. Henry Pen 28 Jan.
William Skinner s. John 11 March
Edward Penny s. John Penny 16 March

1654.

William Baker s. Christopher 29 March
Jane Good d. Henry 2 April
Robert King s. John 2 April
Elizabeth Randoll d. Alexander 20 May
John Scammell s. John 20 June
Jane Scud d. Tho. Scud *alias* Gilbird 26 July
Jane Norris d. Henry 7 Aug.
Jane Guyer d. John 26 Aug.
John White s. Henry 28 Aug.
Samuell Penny s. Christopher 10 Oct.
Jane ffrancis d. Nicholas 18 Nov.
William Wag s. John 21 Nov.
Timothy Harris s. Timothy 30 Jan.
Samuell Lilly s. Samuell 1 Feb.
William Chalke s. Edward 19 Feb.
Elizabeth White d. Jeffery 22 Feb.
Henry Harris s. John, keeper, 5 March
Edith Randoll d. John Randoll 11 March

1655.

Rachell Lodge d. Timothy Lodge 1 April
Margaret Skinner d. John Skinner 7 Ap.
Elizabeth Harvie d. Edmond Harvie April
Thomas Bydlecomb s. Edward Bydlecomb April
Jane Odber d. William Odber 19 April
Richard Spencer s. Richard 23 April
John Miles s. Cornelius Miles 18 May
John Dew s. Thomas Dew 16 July
Anna Diblen d. George
Mary Grove d. William Grove gen. 18 July
Mary Read d. Thomas Read 22 July
Elizabeth Holly d. William 18 Aug.
Anne Sloper d. John Sloper, Vicar, 18 Aug.
Mary Archer d. Anthony 8 Sep.

William Pitchland s. William 10 Sep.
Sara Huntly d. Michaell 1 Oct.
Samuell White s. Thomas 31 Oct.
John Cooper s. John Cooper 4 Feb.
John Brookman s. Arthur Brookman 11 Nov.
William Angood s. Henry Angood 28 Nov.
Jane Bennet d. Thomas 17 Jan.
Henry Quintyn s. Henry Quintyn 5 Feb.
Mary Witt d. Cornelius 26 Feb.
Moses Bundy s. John 3 March
Sara White d. Henry 9 March
Anna King d. Robert King 13 March
Elizabeth Orchard d. Richard 17 March
Margaret King d. William 24 March

1656.

Elizabeth Wagge d. Richard 2 June
Mary Whitmarsh d. William 3 July
Jane Penny d. Christopher Oct.
Alexander ffolliat s. John 25 Oct.
John White s. Jeffery 5 Dec.
Dionize Skinner d. John 10 Dec.
Jane Notte d. Nicholas 28 Jan.
Margaret Sanders d. John 2 Feb.
William Spencer s. Richard 8 Feb.
Charles Harris s. John, keeper, 16 Feb.

1657.

John Bundy s. John 6 April
Alexander King s. Samuell 18 April
Mary Deane d. William 4 May
John Good s. Henry de Moul 31 May
Henry Penny s. Henry 1 July
Joane Scud *alias* Gylberd d. Thomas 30 July
Sara Lodge d. Anthony 7 Sep.
Elizabeth ffrancis d. Alexander 16 Sep.
Edmond Harvie s. Edmond 26 Sep.
Thomas Jeffery s. Robert 31 July
John White s. John 27 Sep.
Luke ffrancis s. Nicholas 18 Oct.
Thomas Penn s. Henry 22 Oct.
Jane Wit d. Cornelius 14 Nov.
Anna Witte d. John 15 Dec.
Margaret Brine d. Edward 14 Dec.
Jane Brookman d. Arthur 19 Dec.

Samuell White s. Henry 18 Dec.
Barbara King d. Robert 21 Jan.
Anna Bydlecomb d. Edward 24 Jan.
Thomas Grove s. William, gent. 24 Jan.

1658.

John Harris s. Timothie 4 April
Mary Grey d. Walter 2 May
Mary Wag d. Richard 13 June
Elizbeth Stockly (?) d. Nicholas 21 June

A gap till

1700.*

Maria Lawes d. George Lawes *bap.* 31
  March
John s. John Street 1 April
Philippa Angood d. William 19 May
Maria d. Gilbert Dod 19 May
Thomas Penny s. John 26 May
John Francis s. John 25 July
Sarah Austen d. Henry 1 Sep.
Thomas Lawes s. Thomas 15 Sep.
William Odbar Savage s. Joseph 18 Oct.
Elizabeth Stickland d. James 1 Nov.
Jane Harvey d. Laurence 17 Nov.
Miles Northover s. John 15 Dec.
William Smith s. David 26 Dec.
Susan Ingram d. Elias 1 Jan.
John Best s. Robert 2 Feb.
Hannah Dean d. Andrew 9 Feb.
Henry King s. Henry 23 Feb.
Jane Cookman d. William 5 March

1701.

John Lawes s. John 13 April
Thomas Fox s. William 17 April
Robert Edmonds s. William 20 April
Thomas King s. Alexander 4 May
Maria Ingram d. John 29 May
Jane Heylock d. John 29 June
Isaac Savage s. Charles 20 July
Elizabeth Randol d. Henry 29 July
William Penny s. William 28 Sep.
Edith Norris d. Henry 28 Sep.
Betty Lawes d. George 23 Nov.
Martha Austen d. Henry†
Anna Penn d. John†
John Best s. Robert†
William Biggs s. William†
Jane Good d. Henry†

1702.

John s. Thomas Scudd 17 April
Elizabeth Hibberd d. William 17 April
Honoria Biddlecomb d. Henry 25 July

* This is again a Register of Baptisms.
† No dates—parchment destroyed by worms.

David Smith s. David 26 July
Elizabeth Fox d. William 2 Aug.
Elizabeth d. Gilbert Dod 4 Oct.
Elizabeth Angood d. William 25 Oct.
James Stickland s. James 25 Oct.
Sarah Ingram d. Elias 15 Nov.
John Cookman s. William 30 Nov.
Thomas nat. s. of Tho. Fish & Susan Miles
  1 Jan.
Maria Antram d. George 6 Jan.
Alexander Scammel s. Thomas *born* 18 Dec.
Thomas Francis s. John *bap*ᵈ 16 Jan.
John Edmonds s. William 24 Jan.
John White s. Abraham 25 Jan.
Susan Penelope Austen d. Henry, Nat.
  Jan. 12 Renat. Feb. 2
John Stent s. Richard, Die Cinerum, 10
  Feb.
George Lawes s. John 1 March
Thomas Dean s. William 3 March

1703.

Thomas Young s. Thomas 18 May
Henry Penny s. Henry 20 June
Jenny Randol d. Henry 11 July
Thomas Northover s. John 12 Sep.
Ralph s. John Street 5 Nov.
William s. Robert Best 12 Dec.
Betty d. Robert Witt 27 Dec.
Henry s. William Penny 28 Dec.
Jane d. Thomas Gilbert 6 Jan.
Eliz* . . . d. Joseph Savage 6 Jan.
Be* . . . bastard child of Elizabeth G . . .
  13 Feb.

1704.

* . . man s. Laurence 27 April
* . . . . s. Thomas 7 May
* . . . . s. William 8 June
* . . . . s. John 29 June.
* . . . . s. Henry *born* 17 July
* . . . . d. David *bap.* 30 July
Maria Stent d. Richard 29 Sep.
Elizabeth Harvey d. Laurence 26 Nov.
Edward Edmonds s. William 3 Dec.
Jane Ingram d. John 28 Dec.
Jane Lawes d. George 7 Jan.
Henry Randal s. Henry 25 Jan.
Daniel Dean s. William 7 March
John Good s. John 7 March
Maria Scammell d. Thomas *born* 29 Feb.

1705.

John Haylock s. John 30 March
Laurence Brookman s. Laurence 17 May
Joan Foxhanger d. William 17 May
Robert Witt s. Robert 3 June

* Worm-eaten.

Anna Young d. Thomas 29 June
Jane Norris d. Henry 29 June
Maria d. John Teape clerici 22 July
Abraham s. Abraham & Deborah White 12 Aug.
John s. John & Mary Folate 21 Sep.
Henry Stickler s. James 29 Sep.
Elizabeth d. George & Mary Antrum 18 Oct.
Margaret d. John & Joyce Penn 18 Oct.
Thomas s. Thomas & Susanna Vincent 25 Jan.
Hannah d. William & Jane Cookman 2 Feb.
Hannah d. Henry & Hannah Penny 24 Feb.
Mary d. Joseph & Anne Savage 8 March

1706.

William s. Thomas & Susanna Fish 6 April
William s. John & Mary Francis*
Robert s. William & Sarah Francis*
Edward s. Robert & Edith Best*
Anne d. William & Jane Penny*
Anne d. Thomas & Anne Street 28 July
Rebecca d. John & Rebecca Lawes 21 Sep.
Anne d. John & Anne Rolfe 14 Nov.
Thomas s. Henry & Eliz. Randoll 24 Nov.
George s. John & Mary Northover 19 Jan.
Thomas s. Thomas & Martha Gilbert 19 Jan.
Harry s. Nicholas & Anne White 22 Jan.
Elizabeth d. Eliz. Read 23 Feb.

1707.

Mary d. James & Catherine Stickler 20 March
Richard s. John & Mary Foliat 30 March
John s. Robert & Joyce Witt 14 April
Hannah d. Thomas & Dinah Young 15 April
Sarah d. John & Jane Littlefield 20 April
James s. David & Jane Smith 2 June
Thomas s. Henry & Sarah Norris 24 June
John s. John & Anne Stockey 29 Aug.
Thomas s. John & Mary Francis 7 Sep.
Elias s. Elias & Anne Ingram 29 Sep.
Robert s. Robert & Elizabeth Bryant 10 Nov.
John s. Thomas & Susan Vincent 17 Nov.
William s. Ambrose & Jane Richards *born* 6 Dec.
William s. William & Sarah Francis bap. 1 Jan.

William s. William & Margaret Penny 20 Jan.
John s. Laurence & Eliz. Brookman 2 Feb.
Mary d. Henry & Hannah Penny 5 March
Robert s. George & Anne Goulden 10 March

1708.

Mary d. Laurence Harvey 5 April
Anne d. Thomas Anne Streete 24 May
Mary d. Henry & Elizabeth Penny 5 June
Thomas s. Nicholas & Anne White 24 June
Robert s. William & Elizabeth F . . . .* 8 Aug.
Robert s. Thomas & Dinah Young 19 Aug.
Benjamin s. William & Joan Young 14 Nov.
Henry s. Henry Ki* . . . . 28 Nov.
Thomas s. John & Rebecca Lawes 28 Nov.
William s. William & Jane Dean 28 Dec.
Thomas s. Gilbert & Mary Dod 6 Jan.
John s. William & Margaret Gould 5 Feb.
Anne d. Thomas & Susanna Fish 2 Feb.
John Harford s. William & Martha Harford 13 March
Thomas s. John & Anne Stockey 16 March.

1709.

Martha d. John & Mary Francis 26 March
Mary d. William & Eliz. Everly 7 April
David s. David & Jane Smith 10 April
Joyce d. Robert & Joyce Witt 25 April
Hannah d. Joseph & Anna Savage 26 April
Nicholas s. John & Mary Foliat 14 June
Henry s. William & Sarah Francis 29 June
William s. Henry & Anne King 3 July
Mary d. Ralph and Mary Good 27 Aug.
John s. John and Anne Rolfe 25 Sep.
Hannah d. Hester Cooke, since wife of John Bodenham, gent. 25 Sep.
Anne d. Richard & Mary Stent 28 Dec.
Harry s. Henry & Catherine Stickler 10 March
Betty d. Jacob & Jane Jennings 15 March

* Worm-eaten.

* Worm-eaten.

1710.

William s. Thomas & Dinah Young 18 May

Elizabeth d. William & Elizabeth Bound 21 May

Edward s. William & Margaret Gould 9 July

Elizabeth d. Laurence & Eliz. Brookman 6 Aug.

Mary d. Ambrose & Anne Roe 1 Aug.

Samuel s. Thomas & Anne Street 21 Sep.

Rebecca d. William & Martha Hartford 15 Oct.

Mary d. Edward & Mary Witt 18 Oct.

Abraham s. Nicholas White 19 Nov.

John Bishop s. Anne Short 17 Dec.

William s. William & Elizabeth Everley 27 Dec.

William s. Thomas & Elinor Vincent 25 Jan.

William s. John & Anne Stockey 10 Feb.

John s. John & Mary Frampton 21 Feb.

Mary d. William & Jane Dean — Feb.

1711.

John s. John & Mary Hunt 25 April

William s. George & Anne Golding 11 June

Jane Penny d. Thomas Penny 31 May

Hannah & Elizabeth twin children of Jn. Lawes 29 July

Elizabeth Biggs d. William — Aug.

Mary d. Jno. Folliot 21 Sep.

Henry s. Henry Williams 21 Sep.

Jane d. Henry & Hannah Penny 26 Sep.

Joseph s. Robert & Joyce Witt 29 Sep.

Henry Laurence s. Henry & Mary 18 Oct.

John s. Thomas & Dinah Young — Nov.

Mary d. John & Mary Northover 26 Oct.

Betty d. Thomas Fish 9 Dec.

Mary d. Edward Fish 1 Jan.

Jane d. Joseph Savage 16 Jan.

John s. David & Jane Smith 2 Feb.

John s. Jacob & Jane Jennings 12 March

Mary d. William & Elizabeth Speering 16 March

1712.

Thomas s. Thomas Penny 5 June

Jane d. Edward & Mary Witt 9 June

John s. Richard Hayward of Stoke 28 Sep.

Thomas s. Ambrose Richards *born* 13 July

William s. William Wray *bap.* 5 Nov.

Henry s. Mary Fish 23 Nov.

Rinald s. Henry Randol 7 Dec.

Jane d. Henry King 1 Jan.

Martha d. William Angood 1 Jan.

John s. Thomas Street 6 Jan.

John s. Jasper Whitmarsh 2 Feb.

Ann d. John Stockey 2 Feb.

. . . . s. Richard Lush 8 March

1713.

William s. John Littlefield 12 April

Robert s. Thomas Young 14 May

Mary d. John Lanham 25 May

John s. Robert Tyler 25 May

William s. William Holmes 11 June

Elizabeth d. Edward Witt 28 June

Martha d. John Follet 25 July

Jane d. Thomas & Jane Penny 16 Aug.

Jane d. Laurence & Elizabeth Brookman 6 Sep.

Thomas s. William & Martha Hartford 20 Sep.

Samuel s. Samuel Penny 27 Sep.

William s. William & Joan Chalk 29 Sep.

Hannah d. Timothy & Hannah Lodge 20 Oct.

Dennis d. Alexander King 26 Oct.

John s. Henry Lawrence *alias* Williams 28 Oct.

Hannah d. James Stickland 28 Oct.

Mary d. John Lawes 8 Nov.

Ann Goulding d. George Goulding 11 Nov.

Alexander Francis s. William Francis 30 Nov.

William s. William Bound 30 Nov.

Elizabeth d. Henry Penny 25 Jan.

1714.

Elizabeth d. William & Elizabeth Wray 30 March

Jane d. John Card 1 May

Martha d. Henry King 1 May

Mary d. Henry Randol 17 May

Abigail d. David Smith 28 May

Edward s. John Frampton 29 June

Thomas s. Henry Cook 29 Sep.

Richard s. Samuel Penny 23 Nov.

William s. Robert Witt 21 Dec.

Jane d. Richard Hayward 2 March

1715.

Robert Bateman Wray s. William & Eliz. Wray 28 March

George & Robert twin children of George Best 11 April

Elizabeth d. Thomas Young 15 April

John s. Elizabeth Andrews 18 April

Ann King d. Alexander King   April

Jane d. William Everley   May

Edward s. Thomas Penny 16 May

William s. William & Eliz. Spearing 17 July

Sarah d. Henry Randol 17 July
Mary d. William Angood 31 July
John s. John Marchant 14 Aug.
Rachel d. Randol Lodge 29 Aug.
Jane d. Ambrose Richards *born* 11 Aug.
Sarah d. Edward Perry *bap.* 9 Oct.
Henry s. John Follet 5 Nov.
Walter s. Walter Whitmarsh 21 Nov.
Dorothy d. Richard Lush 30 Nov.
George s. George Golden 30 Nov.
Edward s. William Chalk 21 Dec.
John s. John Lanham 2 Feb.
Jane d. Edward Penny 7 Feb.
Sarah d. George Laws 15 Feb.
Mary d. John Stockey 24 Feb.
Mary d. Timothy Lodge 29 Feb.
Ann d. Jasper Whitemarsh 2 March
Ann d. Jacob Jennings 16 March

1716.

Mary d. Henry Williams 31 March
Mary d. Thomas Street 15 April
Thomas s. Thomas Batt 14 June
Patience d. Phœbe Rains 15 July
William s. William Langtry 6 Sep.
Jane d. James Stickler 29 Sep.
Ann d. Richard Roberts 30 Sep.
Samuel & Thomas twin children of Samuel
    White 30 Oct.
Sarah d. Alexander King 5 Nov.
Elizabeth d. Charles Miles 12 Nov.
Nicholas s. Nicholas White 19 Nov.
John s. Henry Cooke 26 Dec.
Jane d. Edward Witt 1 Jan.
George s. Mary Frampton, widow, 6 Jan.
David s. John Lawes 3 Feb.
Mary d. Thomas Ingram 6 March
George s. George Turner 13 March

1717.

Jane d. Arthur Hopkins 27 March
Thomas s. Thomas Smith 3 April
Thomas s. Thomas Penny 14 April
Edward s. Robert Witt 22 April
Ann d. Randol Lodge 3 May
Joseph s. Thomas Vincent 24 June
Henry s. William Biggs 29 June
Margaret Ann d. William & Elizabeth
    Wray 4 Sep.
John s. David Skinner 18 Sep.
Mary d. Francis & Mary Plank 25 Sep.
Lucy d. Edward Perry — Oct.
Thomas s. Thomas Wagg 18 Oct.
Henry s. Henry King 25 Nov.
Martha d. William Speering 11 Dec.
David s. Richard Roberts 22 Dec.

Mary d. Thomas Young 8 Jan.
Jacob s. Jacob Jennings 12 Feb.
Walter s. John Foliot 16 March

1718.

Henry s. John Stockey 26 March
William s. William Langtry 26 March
Mary d. George Clark 16 April
Hannah d. Edward Savage 16 April
Jane d. Walter Whitmarsh 30 April
Joseph s. Henry Randol 20 May
Mary d. Henry Randol 20 May
Mary d. Thomas Penny 8 June
Mary d. of a Traveller 13 July
Edith d. Robert Best 16 July
Jane d. George Turner 3 Aug.
Mary d. John Lewin 3 Aug.
John s. Thomas Batt 13 Aug.
Charles s. William & Elizabeth Wray
    2 Sep.
William s. William & Dinah Lilly 28 Sep.
Sarah d. William Viney 29 Oct.
Charles s. William Hartford 30 Oct.
Mary d. Alexander King 5 Nov.
Sarah d. Richard Stent 26 Nov.
Ann d. Arthur Hopkins 3 Dec.
Mary d. Randol Lodge 9 Dec.
John s. John Angood 15 Dec.
Edward s. Richard Lush — Dec.
* ... es s. Edward Penny
* ..... d. Jasper Whitmarsh 11 Feb.
* ..... s. Samuel White — Feb.
* ..... d. David Skinner 10 March

1719.

* ..... s. Lawrence Brookman 29 April
* ..... s. George Golding 27 May
* ..... d. William Chalk 27 May
Catherine d. Edward Witt 25 July
Philip s. John Laws 2 Aug.
Jane d. Wm. Angood 21 Aug.
John s. Elizabeth King 23 Sep.
William s. Henry Cook 29 Sep.
Ruth d. Thomas Penny 11 Oct.
Robert s. Stephen Hort 5 Nov.
Henry s. John Lanham 9 Dec.
John s. Richard Hawkins 13 Dec.
John s. William Lilly 16 Dec.
William s. Edward Perry 16 Dec.
Martha d. William Biggs 1 Jan.
Anthony s. Anthony Penny 16 Jan.
Mary d. Thomas Wagg 2 Feb.
Jane d. Henry King 7 Feb.
Bridget d. Thomas Smith 17 Feb.
Thomas s. George Turner — Feb.

* Worm-eaten.

Mary d. William & Elizabeth Wray — Feb.
John s. William Speering 6 March

1720.

Ann d. John Foliot 18 April
Jane d. Thomas Ingram 15 May
Jane d. Edward Harvey 21 Aug.
Elizabeth d. Thomas Penny 9 Sep.
William s. Thomas Moody 1 Dec.
John s. Samuel Penny *
Sarah d. Thomas Wilkins *
Mary d. Robert Best *
Roger s. Roger Barnes *
Edward s. John Angood *
Joyce d. John Stockey — Feb.
Richard s. David Skinner — March
Joseph s. Edward Savage — March
Hannah d. Richard Lush — March

1721.

Margaret d. Jacob Jennings 8 April
Sarah d. William Chalk 3 May
Ann d. Richard Roberts 14 May
Hannah d. Alexander King 9 June
John s. Thomas Laws 5 July
Eleanor d. Charles Gould 12 July
John s. George Laws 13 Sep.
Mary d. Stephen Hort 18 Oct.
Mary Morgan d. John Argus 15 Nov.
Ann d. Samuel Penny 23 Nov.
John s. Richard Barter 10 Jan.
John s. Anthony Penny 5 Feb.
John s. Edward Harvy 25 Feb.

1722.

William s. Edward Witt 2 May
Jonathan s. John Foliot 29 May
George s. George Reed 13 June
Lucy d. Edward Perry 19 June
Robert s. Thomas Moody 28 June
Dennis d. Jasper Whitmarsh 11 July
Martha d. William Speering 25 July
Mary d. William Bound 19 Sep.
Elizabeth d. Henry King 24 Oct.
Martha d. Henry Cook 24 Oct.
Robert s. Philippa Angood 10 Dec.
Richard s. Richard King —— Dec.
William s. John Angood

1723.

Esther d. Charles Garret 29 May
Elizabeth d. Edward Harvey 2 June
Elisabeth d. Robert Best 9 June
John s. Thomas Wagg 9 June
Jacob s. Jacob Jennings 16 June
Henry s. John Barter 10 July
Elisabeth d. Thomas Smith 4 Aug.

* Worm-eaten.

Anne d. George Reed 18 Sep.
Mary d. Roger Barnes 27 Nov.
William s. William Lilly 15 Dec.
Stephen s. Steven Hort 5 Jan.
George s. Henry Randol 17 Jan.
James s. Edward Savage 11 March
Jane d. William Langtry 24 March

1724.

Amy d. John Argus 25 March
Margaret d. Randol Lodge 8 April
William s. Richard King 26 April
Lucy d. Alexander King 14 June
Elizabeth d. John Day 28 June
Jane d. Henry Stainer 15 July
John s. Thomas Mighel 2 Sep.
Ann d. Jeremiah Bailee 3 Sep.
Joseph ille. s. Mary Shank of the parish
    of Gusedge, in the county of Dorset,
    4 Sep.
Charles s. William Smith 9 Sep.
Hannah d. John Stockey 24 Sep.
John s. William Biggs 29 Sep.
Mary d. Thomas Ingram 14 Oct.
Elizabeth d. Thomas Smith 30 Oct.
Mary d. Edward Perry 5 Nov.
William s. Joseph Whitmarsh 16 Dec.
Patience d. Edward Witt 29 Dec.
William s. Thomas Moody 21 Jan.
Mary d. Edward Penny 2 Feb.
John s. Edward Harvey 17 Feb.
Milian d. John Angood 17 Feb.
Elizabeth d. Richard Barter 19 Feb.

1725.

Mary d. Anthony Penny 25 March
William s. Samuel Penny 5 May
George s. George & Sarah Read 2 June
Thomas s. David & Jane Skinner 16 June
George s. Henry & Elisabeth Randol 4
    July
Charles s. Thomas & Elisabeth Batt 28
    July
Elizabeth d. John & Mary Foliat 15 Aug.
Henry s. Henry & Jane King 10 Oct.
Mary d. John Powell 27 Dec.
Jenny d. Richard King 13 Feb.
Ann d. Robert Best 16 Feb.
Robert s. Roger Barnes 16 Feb.
Mary d. Henry Cook 4 March
John s. John Laws 6 March

1726.

John Lodge s. Mary Jennings 26 March
Edith d. Randolph Lodge 11 April
William s. George Autram 13 April
Sarah & Susanna dd. Eliz. Speering 8 May
Mary d. Peregrine & Mary Dove 22 May

Thomas s. Stephen & Mary Hort 19 June
John Butler s. John Butler & Elisabeth
Gold 13 Aug.
Charles s. William & Elisabeth Smith 17
Aug.
Jane d. Thomas & Jane Ingram 28 Aug.
Elizabeth d. Tho. & Jane Laws 19 Nov.
Amy Penruddock 22 Dec.
Mary d. Edward & Judith Savage 27 Dec.
Mary d. Tho. Mighell 11 Jan.
Elizabeth d. John Cole gent. 12 Jan.

1727.

Hannah d. Edward Harvey 26 March
Sarah d. John Powell 30 April
John s. John Biggs 16 May
William s. Thomas Batt 5 July
George s. David Skinner 5 July
Sarah d. Richard & Elisabeth Barter 25
Aug.
Henry s. John & Mellier Angood 30 Aug.
Thomas s. George & Sarah Read 17 Sep.
Mary d. James & Joyce Stickland 18 Sep.
John s. Thomas & Mary Ingram 22 Oct.
Jane d. Anthony & Jane Penny 30 Oct.
William s. William & Anne Williams 8
Nov.
Robert s. Thomas & Anne Moody 16 Nov.
Edith d. William & Edith Angood 3 Dec.
Thomas s. Jane Cookman 7 Dec.
John s. John & Elisabeth Gibbs 25 Dec.
Alice d. Edward & Alice Perry 7 Feb.
James s. Ralph & Ruth Streight 11 Feb.
Anne d. Henry & Jane King 11 Feb.
Joseph s. Thomas & Mary Smith 16 Feb.

1728.

William s. William & Mary King 17 June
Elisabeth d. Robert & Elisabeth Merchant
24 July
Mary d. Thomas & Mary King 18 Aug.
Hannah d. John & Hannah Laws 18 Sep.
Roger s. Roger & Margaret Beling 13
Oct.
Sarah d. Robert & Edith Best 16 Oct.
Henry s. Henry & Martha Cook 29 Nov.
Eliz. d. Tho. & Hester Jolliffe 1 Dec.
James s. Stephen & Mary Hort 22 Dec.
Anne d. John & Anne Grey 29 Dec.
Anne d. John & Mary Powell 19 Jan.
Mary d. William & Anne Williams 26
Jan.
Mary Noise bast. d. Jane Dewe 31 Jan.
Anthony s. Thomas & Jane Ingram 9
Feb.
Betty d. Walter & Joyce Beling 14 Feb.
Stephen s. William & Elisabeth Smith 23
Feb.

1729.

Osmyn s. Osmyn & Mary Martin 15 April
Edward s. Samuel & Anne Penny 20
April
Aimis d. Richard & Elisabeth Barter 4
May
Anne d. William & Mary Laws 26 June
Elisabeth d. Anthony & Jane Penny 8
July
Sarah d. Thomas & Jane Laws 10 July
William & Mary children of Henry & Jane
Stainer 7 Sep.
Mary d. David & Jane Skinner 24 Sep.
Henry s. James & Joyce Strickland 1 Oct.
Bethiah d. Roger & Elisabeth Barns 26
Nov.
Thomas s. George & Sarah Read 6 Jan.
Mary d. John & Elisabeth Gibbs 20 Jan.
Moses bast. s. Honour Biddlecome 2 Feb.
John s. Robert & Elisabeth Merchant 25
Feb.

1730.

Mary d. William & Mary King 25 April
Richard s. Richard & Betty Foliat 24 May
William s. Thomas & Esther Jolliffe 26
July
John s. Richard & Mary Johnson 2 Aug.
Hannah d. John & Mary Powel 8 Nov.
John s. Thomas & Mary Smith 2 Dec.
John s. Roger & Margaret Beling 10 Jan.
Elias s. George & Sarah Read 16 Jan.
Mary d. John & Hannah Laws 7 March
John s. William & Anne Williams 7 March

1731.

John bast. s. Elizabeth Speering 19 April
Henry s. Henry & Mary Penn 27 May
Mary Anne d. Osmyn & Mary Martin 18
July
Mary d. Richard & Elisabeth Barter 25
July
Hannah d. Philip & Mary Kirley 15 Aug.
George s. William & Mary Laws 25 Aug.
Susanna d. Joseph & Eleanor Combes 27
Aug.
Mary d. Robert & Mary Fox 31 Aug.
Mary d. William & Mary Hewlet 12 Sep.
Charles s. Thomas & Elisabeth Batt 1
Nov.
Edward s. Henry & Martha Cook 1 Nov.
Mary d. Laurence & Elisabeth Thick 5
Nov.
Zechariah s. Jeremiah & Mary Baily 14
Nov.
Joyce d. Walter & Joyce Beling 21 Nov.
Jane d. Thomas & Jane Laws 6 Jan.

James s. James & Joyce Strickland 19 Jan.
Robert s. Robert & Elisabeth Merchant 2 Feb.
Anne d. John & Elisabeth Gibbs 13 Feb.
Betty d. Richard & Betty Foliot 5 March
George s. Mr Roger & Elisabeth Barns 16 March

1732.

Martha d. John & Mary Powel 7 April
George s. William & Elisabeth Northover 25 April
Mary d. John & Patience Martin 9 July
John s. Thomas & Esther Jollyffe 25 July
Jane d. William & Mary King 6 Aug.
Robert s. Robert & Mary Fox 1 Oct.
Mary d. William & Jane Langtry 24 Oct.
Lucy d. Philip & Mary Kirley 10 Dec.
James s. John & Hannah Laws 17 Dec.
Elisabeth d. Thomas & Susanna Laws 28 Jan.
Sarah d. George & Mary Northover 18 Feb.
Elisabeth d. Henry & Christiane Kerley 11 March
Hannah d. James & Joyce Strickland 23 March

1733.

Rebecca d. Robert & Edith Best 25 March
Mary d. Miles & Elisabeth Northover 1 May
Ruth d. William Frecker & Philippe 10 June
Anne d. Thomas & Anne Hesket 11 June
Mary d. William & Sarah Hayward 29 June
Jane bast. d. Jinny Penny 29 Sep.
Anne d. Richard & Elisabeth Barter 7 Oct.
Thomas s. Henry & Mary Penn 1 Nov.
John bast. s. Anne Stent 30 Nov.
Sarah d. Richard & Monica Jolliff 26 Dec.

1734.

Elisabeth d. William & Elisabeth Scammel 10 April
Elisabeth d. John & Elisabeth Gibbs — May
Sarah d. Thomas & Mary Smith 1 Sep.
Henry s. David & Anne Smith 8 Sep.
Sarah d. Thomas & Anne Hesket 15 Sep.
Jane & Roger s. and d. Thomas & Esther Jollyffe 5 Oct.
Mary d. Richard & Betty Folliot 18 Oct.
George s. George & Mary Northover 28 Oct.

William s. Mr William & Mary Gifford 28 Oct.
John s. John & Mary Yates 21 Jan.
William s. John & Mary Powel 25 Jan.
Joseph s. Joseph & Eleanor Combes 2 March

1735.

Mary d. Robert & Mary Fox 25 April
Thomas s. William & Mary Hewlet 1 May
John s. Samuel & Elisabeth King 25 May
Sarah d. William & Mary King 26 May
James s. Thomas & Elisabeth Moody 15 June
John s. John & Mary Barnet 15 July
Mary d. Henry & Christiane Kirley 20 July
Sarah d. Gehazi & Anne Baker 10 Aug.
Mary d. Jeremiah & Mary Baily 31 Aug.
Esther d. William & Philippe Frecker 28 Sep.
Sarah d. William & Sarah Haywood 4 Nov.
Sarah d. John & Hannah Laws 5 Nov.
John s. William & Sarah Butcher 27 Dec.
Thomas s. Thomas & Jane Laws 6 Jan.
Stephen s. David & Anne Smith 12 Jan.
Anne d. Charles & Mary Hiscock 28 Jan.
Ralph s. Henry & Mary Penny 11 Feb.
Miles s. Miles & Elisabeth Northover 7 March
Sarah d. John & Elisabeth Gibs 14 March
Sarah d. William & Betty Scammel 17 March

1736.

Mary d. Mr William & Mary Gifford 6 April
Miles s. John & Mary Powel 9 May
Elizabeth d. William & Elisabeth Northover 29 May
William bast. s. Jane Smith 14 June
John s. John & Elisabeth Young 24 June
William s. Thomas & Elisabeth Vincent 27 June
Elisabeth d. Jonathan & Jane Roberts 29 June
James s. George & Elisabeth Northover 1 Aug.
Jane d. James & Joyce Strickland 2 Sep.
Richard s. Richard & Elisabeth Barter 17 Oct.
Benjamin s. Robert & Edith Best 12 Dec.
Sarah d. David & Anne Smith 27 Dec.
Honour d. William & Honour Viny 6 Feb.
John Laurence s. Charles & Mary Hiscock 27 Feb.

Christopher s. William & Martha Penny 6 March
Miles s. Miles & Elisabeth Northover 15 March

1737.

William s. Robert Fox & Mary 27 March
Richard s. Richard & Betty Folliot 30 May
Anne d. John & Milliere Angood 5 June
George s. William & Mary King 3 July
Caleb s. Caleb & Tabitha Cavil 10 July
Aimée bast. d. Mary Harvey 10 July
Thomas s. George & Mary Northover 24 July
Jane d. Thomas & Mary Gold 31 July
Mary d. John & Martha Merchant 21 Sep.
Christiane d. Henry & Christiane Kirley 12 Nov.
John s. John & Honour Pin 20 Nov.
Jane d. Aaron & Jane Thompson 20 Nov.
Mary d. George & Anne Laws 11 Dec.
Sarah d. William & Sarah Haywood 18 Dec.
Anne d. William & Mary Hewlet 8 Jan.
Luke s. Luke & Esther Francis 15 Jan.
Anne d. Thomas & Esther Jollyff 15 Jan.
Mary d. James & Anne Chaunt 25 Jan.
John s. Thomas & Anne Hesket 19 Feb.
Thomas s. Thomas & Elisabeth Vincent 19 Feb.
John s. John & Mary Abbot 12 March

1738.

Martha d. John & Elisabeth Gibs 5 April
Hannah d. Nicholas & Hannah White 9 April
Susanna d. Thomas & Rebecca Read 11 April
John s. Jonathan & Jane Roberts 23 May
Henry s. William & Sarah Butcher 29 May
Jane d. Mr William & Mary Gifford 22 Aug.
Joseph s. Benjamin & Jane Johnson 26 Aug.
Charles s. Mr Charles & Elisabeth Chanliss 20 Sep.
George s. Robert & Mary Fox 1 Oct.
Thomas s. John & Jane Witt 5 Nov.
Jane d. David & Anne Smith 6 Dec.
Mary d. Samuel & Diana King 29 Dec.
Matthew Frampton bast. s. Elisabeth Brookman 2 Jan.
Jane d. William & Elisabeth Northover 7 March

1739.

William s. Richard & Jane Lush 8 April
William s. John Everett & Anne 23 April
Mary d. Thomas & Edith Cook 6 May
John s. Philip & Martha Kirley 24 June
Josiah s. Thomas & Mary Gold 26 June
Mary d. John & Jane Penny 8 July
Betty d. William & Mary King 9 Sep.
William s. John & Hannah Laws 29 Sep.
George s. John & Mary Abbot 7 Oct.
Samuel s. Caleb & Tabitha Cavil 11 Oct.
Betty d. John & Martha Merchant 21 Oct.
Elisabeth d. James & Joyce Strickland 11 Nov.
Jane d. Thomas & Elisabeth Vincent 16 Dec.
John bastard s. Jane Humphreys 20 Jan.
Martha d. of Richard & Betty Folliot 20 Jan.
Henry s. John & Honour Pin 27 Jan.
John s. Robert & Jane Golding 20 Feb.
Jane bastard d. Ann Feltham 25 Feb.
Sarah d. Thomas & Rebecca Read 4 Mar.

1740.

Esther d. Luke & Esther Francis 30 Mar.
Henry s. Nicholas & Hannah White 28 May
Robert s. John & Anne Williams 27 June
Rose d. John & Elizabeth Young 29 June
Robina d. John & Jane Witt 29 June
Mary d. James & Anne Smith 7 July
John s. John & Jane Whittridge 27 July
David s. Jonathan & Jane Roberts 17 Aug.
James s. Charles & Mary Hiscock 31 Aug.
Anne d. Mr William & Mary Gifford 4 Sep.
Stephen s. Robert & Mary Fox 12 Oct.
James s. Richard & Elisabeth Barter 30 Oct.
Henry s. Aaron & Jane Thompson 2 Nov.
Elisabeth d. Thomas & Mary Barfoot 29 Dec.
Anne d. David & Anne Smith 4 Jan.
Jane d. John & Anne Everett 6 Jan.
William s. George & Elizabeth Turner 25 Jan.

1741.

John s. James & Anne Smith 18 May
George & Elizabeth s. and d. Elias & Elisabeth Ingram 26 July
William s. William & Anne Stevens 27 July
John s. William & Elisabeth Barret 30 Sep.
William s. William & Elisabeth Northover 11 Oct.
Robert s. John & Mary Perry 15 Nov.

Charles s. Thomas & Rebecca Read 6 Jan.
Sarah d. John & Honour Pin 24 Feb.
Mary d. Richard & Jane Lush 3 March
Martha d. Thomas & Elisabeth Vincent
  11 March

1742.

Mary d. John & Jane Witt 25 March
William s. John & Jane Vettridge
James s. Joseph & Eleanor Combs 16 April
Sarah d. Caleb & Tabitha Cavil 19 April
William s. William & Mary King 5 May
Rebecca d. Edward & Susanna Witt 24
  June
Henry bastard s. Martha Savage 29 June
Bravant s. Bravant & Mary West 18 July
Martha d. Gyles & Martha Pickford (?)
  25 July
Anne d. John & Elizabeth Young 24 Aug.
Robert s. Robert & Jane Golding 10 Oct.
Betty d. Robert & Mary Fox 11 Oct.
George s. George & Elisabeth Turner 1
  Nov.
Elisabeth d. David & Anne Smith 14 Nov.
William s. Benjamin & Jane Johnson 19
  Dec.
John s. John & Martha Perry 16 Jan.
John s. Luke & Esther Francis 23 Jan.
William s. Samuel & Diana King 13 Mar.

1743.

Mary d. William & Mary Crine 10 April
Jane d. William & Mary Hewlet 31 July
John s. Antony & Grace Penny 14 Aug.
James s. James & Anne Smith 18 Sep.
James s. Charles & Anne Silcock 18 Sep.
Elias s. Elias & Elisabeth Ingram 29 Sep.
Thomas bastard s. Mary Ingram 23 Oct.
Anne d. William & Sarah King 22 Jan.
John s. John & Jane Witt 25 Jan.
Ether s. Richard & Jane Lush 12 Feb.
Jane d. John & Jane Vettridge 12 Feb.
Mary d. John & Anne Everett 26 Feb.
James & John ss. John & Mary Dibben
  28 Feb.

1744.

John s. John & Mary Chaunt 25 March
Robert & Thomas ss. William & Elisabeth
  Northover 25 March
George s. Thomas & Rebecca Read 23
  April
William s. William & Martha Penny 16
  May
John s. Thomas & Mary Gold 17 June
Joseph s. Bravall & Mary West 17 June
John s. Caleb & Tabitha Cavil 29 June
Thomas s. George & Elisabeth Turner 25
  July

Sarah d. Henry & Elisabeth Jay 5 Aug.
Nicolas s. Nicolas & Hannah White 29
  Sep.
Susanna d. Edward & Susanna Witt 27
  Oct.
James s. John & Elisabeth Young 28 Oct.
Stephen s. William & Mary Crine 1 Nov.
Sarah d. Thomas & Mary Moody 11 Nov.
Stephen s. Robert & Mary Fox 30 Nov.
William s. William & Anne Stephens 2
  Feb.
John s. Joseph & Eleanor Combs 9 March

1745.

Abraham s. Henry & Hannah White 12
  April
Susana d. Thomas & Elisabeth Vincent 15
  April
Betty bastard d. Mary King 16 April
Charles s. Charles & Mary Hiscock 25
  April
Thomas s. William & Elisabeth Northover
  29 June
George s. Elias & Elisabeth Ingram 14
  July
Mary d. John & Bridget Perry 25 July
Ruth d. John & Honour Pin 4 Aug.
William s. John & Mary Dibben 15 Aug.
Thomas s. Henry & Elisabeth Jay 29 Sep.
Henry s. William & Sarah King 29 Sep.
William s. Benjamin & Jane Johnson 3
  Nov.
Mary d. Robert & Jane Golding 17 Nov.
Thomas s. Thomas & Mary Moody 21
  Nov.
Elisabeth d. Luke & Esther Francis 1 Dec.
Anne d. John & Anne Everet 25 Jan.
George s. William & Elisabeth King 23
  Feb.
Betty d. John & Jane Witt 24 Feb.
Betty d. George & Elisabeth Turner 2
  March
John s. George & Mary Sansom 9 Mar.
Elisabeth d. Roger & Anne Barns 9 March

1746.

Mary d. William & Jane Langtry 1 April
Sarah d. Caleb & Tabitha Cavil 22 May
John s. John & Jane Roaf 25 May
Anstice d. John & Elisabeth Young 8
  June
Mary d. Antony & Grace Penny 15 June
Nathanael s. William & Mary Crine 30
  July
Sarah d. Luke & Jane Taylour 31 Aug.
Henry bastard s. Mary Ingram 14 Sep.
Thomas s. Thomas & Rebecca Read 9 Oct.

Sarah d. William & Mary Hewlet 7 Dec.
Joseph s. John & Briget Perry 14 Dec.
William s. William & Sarah King 1 Mar.
Mary d. Charles & Mary Hiscook 4 March

1747.

Sarah d. Thomas & Mary Gold 25 March
William* s. William & Jane Langtry 5
.   April
Catharine d. Nicolas & Hannah White
25 April
George s. Henry & Hannah White 24 May
John s. John & Elisabeth Cook 7 June
Mary d. John & Elisabeth Emme 29 Aug.
Mary d. Thomas & Mary Turner 6 Dec.
Charles s. John & Mary Hazil 2 Nov.
John s. Benjamin & Jane Johnson 17 Jan
John s. John & Anne Everet 30 Jan.
Joseph s. Thomas & Elisabeth Vincent 2
Feb.
Sarah d. John & Mary Dibbens 7 Feb.
Stephen s. Henry & Elisabeth Jay 14 Feb.
William s. Luke & Esther Francis 6 Mar.

1748.

Edward s. Edward & Mary Presly 27 Mar.
Mary d. Thomas & Susanna Laws 27 Mar.
Sarah d. Thomas & Elisabeth Emme 27
Mar.
Joseph s. John & Honour Pin 9 April
William s. Stephen & Mary Smith 11
April
Richard s. Richard & Jane Lush 5 June
Sarah d. William & Jane Langtry 7 July
Anne d. Antony & Grace Penny 11 Sep.
Henry s. William & Mary Crine 11 Sep.
Martha d. Samuel & Diana King 23 Sep.
John s. William & Sarah King 25 Sep.
John s. John & Jane Grey 2 Oct.
Betty d. John & Betty Young 10 Oct.
Mary d. John & Mary Chaunt 23 Oct.
Rebecca d. Thomas & Martha Heydon 27
Nov.
Jane d. Robert & Jane Golding 27 Nov.
William s. Caleb & Tabitha Cavil 26 Dec.
Mary d. John & Elisabeth Cook 22 Jan.
William s. John & Martha Merchant 5
Feb.
George s. George & Mary Sansum 12 Feb.
Sarah d. John & Anne Williams 19 Mar.

1749.

Susanna d. Thomas & Rebecca Read 30
Mar.
Stephen s. John & Mary Dibbens 22 April
Robert s. John & Bridget Perry 30 April

* Note in Register : " Clerk of the Parish in
1826."

Joseph s. John & Jane Witt 25 June
Betty bastard d. Jane Langtry 23 July
Grace d. Thomas & Mary Gold 6 Aug.
Sarah d. William & Jane Langtry 13 Aug.
James s. Thomas & Mary Turner 2 Dec.
Jane d. Stephen & Mary Smith 3 Dec.
Betty d. John & Elisabeth Emme 5 Jan.
Betty d. Charles & Mary Hiscock 7 Jan.
Jane d. John & Jane Roaf 28 Feb.
Charles s. William & Mary Stephens 10
Mar.

1750.

Henry s. John & Mary Hazel 1 April
Henry s. John & Anne Everet 1 April
John s. John & Mary Barter 1 April
George s. William & Mary Hewlet 29
April
Joseph s. Thomas & Elisabeth Emme 29
April
Lucy d. John & Honour Pin 29 April·
John s. Henry & Elisabeth Jay 25 July
Sarah d. Thomas & Elisabeth Vincent 5
Aug.
Joseph s. Ralph & Ruth Street 16 Sep.
James s. Benjamin & Jane Johnson 28
Oct.
Betty d. Robert & Jane Penny 25 Nov.
Harry s. John & Betty Cook 27 Dec.
George s. William & Sarah King 23 Dec.
Martha & Mary dd. John & Jane Smith,
travellers, 24 Jan.
James s. William & Jane Langtry, 24
March

1751.

William s. William & Elisabeth King 12
April
Charles s. William & Martha Penny 20
April
Sarah d. George & Mary Sansom 27 May
John s. Samuel & Diana King 14 July
Sarah d. John & Mary Dibbens 14 July
William s. John & Mary Hasel 21 July
Jeams s. John & Mary Powel 19 Aug.
George s. Robert & Jane Golden 1 Sep.
Thomas s. Thomas & Marthar Haiden
5 Sep.
Elizabeth d. John & Anne Williames 13
Oct.
Jeams s. John & Bidjet Perry 27 Oct.
Lucy d. John & Mary Barter 22 Nov.
Mary d. John & Elizabeth Emme 26 Dec.

1752.

Anne d. Robert & Jane Penny 14 Jan.
Mary d. Caleb & Tabita Cavil 13 March
Charles s. Stephen & Mary Smith 16 Aug.

John s. William & Mary Tudgey 1 Sep.
Elizabeth d. Daniel & Betty Thompson 1 Oct.
Mary d. John & Elizabeth Emme 10 Dec.
Jane Langtree d. William & Jane 17 Dec.

1753. (N. S.)

Mary d. John & Mary Powel 5 Jan.
John s. John & Elizabeth King 21 Jan.
Mary Smith base-born d. Mary King 11 Feb.
Mary d. George & Mary Sansom 25 Feb.
Anne d. Thomas & Betty Gould 27 March
Mary d. Edward & Anne Hardyman 1 April
John s. Thomas & Mary Batchelor 4 April
John s. John & Jane Toomer 24 April
Betty d. John & Ann Everet 3 June
Thomas s. Luke & Esther Francis 10 June
Grace d. Anthony & Grace Penny 11 June
James s. John & Bridget Perry 11 June
William s. John & Elizabeth Emme 12 June
Sarah d. Henry & Hannah White 28 Oct.
Mary d. Henry & Elizabeth Jay 23 Dec.

1754.

William s. Robert & Jane Golding 20 Jan.
Thomas s. John & Betty Cook 3 Mar.
Thomas s. Benjamin & Jane Johnson 3 March
George s. John & Mary Lawes 20 March
James s. William & Mary Tudgey 20 April
Henry s. John & Mary Dibben 2 June
Ann d. John & Ann Williams 3 June
Sarah d. John & Jane Toomer 7 July
William s. Thomas & Alice Teague 4 Aug.
John s. Edward & Anne Hardyman 8 Sep.
John s. Edward & Mary Angood 21 Sep.
William s. Thomas & Elizabeth Cook 22 Sep.
Samuel, base-born, s. Ann Lawes 27 Oct.
Harry s. Robert & Jane Penny 3 Nov.
Thomas s. Thomas & Mary Batchelor 24 Nov.
Mary d. Daniel & Elizabeth Thompson 24 Nov.
Thomas s. George & Mary Sansom 1 Dec.
Joseph s. John & Honour Pin 26 Dec.

1755.

Lucy d. Samuel & Mary Prestly (Travellers) 26 Jan.
John s. David & Ann Gerard 8 March
Harry s. William & Elizabeth King 8 Mar.
Elizabeth d. Thomas & Elizabeth Emme 13 April

Elizabeth d. William & Jane Langtree 13 April
Rose (base-born) d. Joyce Beling 4 May
Betty d. John & Ann Everet 29 June
Deborah d. Thomas & Mary Gould 13 July
James s. Henry & Mary Strickland 27 July
Joshua s. Stephen & Mary Smith 31 Aug.
Jenny d. Richard & Jane Lush 21 Sep.
James s. Christopher & Eleanor Stone 28 Sep.
Mary d. William & Elizabeth Shepherd 5 Oct.
Thomas s. John & Jane Witt 1 Nov.
Esau s. Thomas & Mary Batchelor 30 Nov.
William s. John & Elizabeth Cook 26 Dec.
William s. William & Mary Tudgey 26 Dec.

1756.

Charles s. John & Mary Dibben 29 Jan.
Harry s. Thomas & Elizabeth Cook 24 Feb.
Sarah d. Charles & Hannah Smith 7 Mar.
John s. John & Mary Lawes 17 Mar.
William s. Anthony & Mary Ingram 28 Mar.
Uriah (base-born) s. Mary Baker 28 Mar.
Elizabeth d. Thomas & Martha Hayden 9 May
Anastase d. John & Ann Williams 7 June
Henry s. William & Elizabeth King 20 June
George s. Henry & Elizabeth Jay 20 June
Daniel s. Caleb & Tabitha Cavil 22 Aug.
George s. Henry & Jane King 12 Sep.
Uretta d. Henry & Hannah White 28 Nov.
Sarah d. Thomas & Elizabeth Cook 12 Dec.
Elizabeth d. William & Elizabeth Shepherd 19 Dec.
John, bastard s. Ann Russel 27 Dec.

1757.

Jeremiah s. Thomas & Alice Teague 7 Jan.
Jane d. Christopher & Eleanor Stone 9 Jan.
James s. William & Jane Langtree 16 Jan.
George s. Robert & Jane Penny 6 Feb.
William s. William & Mary James 8 April
Ann d. Robert & Jane Golding 11 April
Jenny d. Mary Mitchel (base-born) 11 April
Mary d. Luke & Esther Francis 15 May
John s. William & Elizabeth Penny 5 June

Sarah d. John & Mary Foyel 28 Aug.
Leah d. Charles & Hannah Smith 4 Sep.
William s. Henry & Elizabeth Jay 25 Sep.
Ann d. John & Jane Grey 25 Sep.
Ann d. Thomas & Elizabeth Emme 9 Oct.
Richard s. William & Mary Tudgey 16 Oct.
Sarah d. John & Bridget Perry 23 Oct.
Mary d. John & Susanna Combes 30 Oct.
Betty d. Anthony & Grace Penny 5 Nov.
Jenny d. Thomas & Alice Teague 18 Dec.

1758.

Elizabeth d. Richard & Sarah Toomer 1 Jan.
Henry-Penny (base-born) s. Martha Gibbs 8 Jan.
Martha d. William & Elizabeth Shepherd 8 Jan.
William s. Daniel & Elizabeth Thompson 5 May
John s. James & Mary Dean 21 May
Christopher s. William & Mary James 21 May
John } twin children of Thomas &
Elizabeth } Judith Trowbridge 21 May
Betty d. John & Mary Stephens 4 June
Harry s. Edward & Mary Angood 30 July
Elizabeth d. John & Elizabeth Cook 6 Aug.
Margaret d. David & Ann Gerard 29 Oct.
Nanny d. John & Grace Grey 3 Dec.

1759.

John s. John & Ann Williams (1) 22 Feb.
William s. John & Mary Dibben (2) 12 Jan.
Nanny d. William & Mary Stephens 24 March
William s. Henry & Mary Strickland 1 April
Mary d. Stephen & Mary Smith 6 April
James s. William & Elizabeth Penny 8 April
Elizabeth d. George & Mary Sansom 27 May
Mary d. Jeremiah & Mary Dowling 4 June
Elizabeth d. William & Elizabeth Shepherd 15 July
Uriah (bastard) s. Mary Barter 10 Aug.
Prudence d. Thomas & Elizabeth Cook 26 Aug.
John s. David & Jane Long 9 Sep.
Betty d. Charles & Hannah Smith 9 Dec.

1760.

Thomas s. John & Jane Grey 13 Jan.
Betty d. William & Elizabeth King 20 Jan.

Thomas s. Thomas & Judith Trowbridge 2 Feb.
Thomas s. Thomas & Mary Batchelor 2 March
Sarah (base-born) d. Mary Mitchel 4 May
James s. Robert & Jane Golding 4 May
Jenny d. Richard & Sarah Toomer 4 May
John s. William & Mary Tudgey 25 May
John s. John & Mary Shepherd 25 May
John s. John & Mary Hibberd 1 Aug.
William s. William & Elizabeth Shepherd 24 Aug.
James s. John & Grace Grey 6 Sep.
Priscilla d. Thomas & Elizabeth Emme 1 Nov.
Henry s. Richard & Jane Read 14 Nov.
Jenny d. Thomas & Elizabeth Foyle 26 Dec.

1761.

Robina d. William & Robina Penny 2 Jan.
Henry s. David & Sarah Long 18 Feb.
Henry s. David & Ann Gerard 24 Feb.
John s. Henry & Elizabeth Penny 24 Mar.
Sarah d. John & Bridget Perry 9 April
Mary d. John & Ann Haskel 11 April
Lucy d. John & Mary Foyle 11 May
Nanny d. Elias & Elizabeth Read 12 May
Elizabeth d. William & Elizabeth Penny 25 May
Rose d. Daniel & Elizabeth Thompson 14 June
John }
Ann } ss. & dd. of John & Elizabeth
Margaret } Emme 1 Aug.
James }
Dinah d. George & Susanna Read 15 Aug.
Susannah d. Thomas & Mary Batchelor 30 Aug.
Thomas s. William & Elizabeth Shepherd 15 Sep.
George s. Richard & Jane Read 19 Sep.
George (base-born) s. Amy Harvey 27 Sep.
William s. William & Mary James 29 Nov.
Eunice d. Henry & Jane King 6 Dec.
Mary d. Thomas & Judith Trowbridge 6 Dec.
Betty d. George & Mary Northover 16 Dec.
Jenny d. Henry & Mary Strickland 21 Dec.
James s. John & Susanna Street 25 Dec.

1762.

James s. William & Mary Tudgey 17 Jan.
Phœbe d. John & Mary Pinn 24 Jan.
Jenny d. Charles & Hannah Smith 9 May
Josiah s. John & Jane Burton 16 May
Catharine d. Thomas & Elizabeth Cook 31 May

Elizabeth d. John & Mary Stephens 1 Aug.
Thomas (base-born) s. Mary Baker 5 Sep.
Thomas s. Thomas & Elizabeth Foyle 12 Sep.
Nanny d. Robert & Ruth Barefoot 17 Dec.
Betty d. Davy & Sarah Long 19 Dec.

1763.

William s. John & Ann Woodland 16 Jan.
Davy s. John & Mary Dibben 10 March
William s. Thomas & Judith Trowbridge 22 March
William s. Jeremiah & Mary Dowling 22 April
Sophia Diana d. George & Mary Northover 6 May
Richard s. Richard & Sarah Toomer 8 Aug.
Sarah d. Ellis & Eliz. Read 16 Aug.
James s. Daniel & Elizabeth Thompson 31 Aug.
Elizabeth d. Richard & Jane Read 19 Nov.
Mary d. Thos. & Mary Vincent 4 Dec.
Richard s. Richard & Sarah Turner 26 Dec.
Sarah d. John & Mary Pinn 26 Dec.

1764.

William s. Henry & Jane King 5 Feb.
George s. Henry & Elizabeth Penny 5 Feb.
John s. John & Jane Burton 5 Feb.
William s. Edward & Mary Angood 26 Feb.
William s. William & Sarah Powel 21 Mar.
James s. John & Mary Hibberd 6 May
Stephen s. Charles & Hannah Smith 9 May
Sarah d. John & Rachel Penny 24 June
James s. Thomas & Elizabeth Foyle 26 Nov.
Sarah d. Rinold & Hannah Randol 17 Dec.

1765.

Elizabeth d. John & Jane Pigot 3 Feb.
Sarah d. Wm & Sarah Lush 22 Feb.
Elizabeth d. John & Mary Hazel 25 Feb.
Betty d. Jeremiah & Mary Dowland 21 April
Wm s. Wm & Betty King 5 May
George s. Thos. & Alice Turner 26 May
James s. John & Ann Woodland 26 May
Henry s. Wm & Robina Penny 16 June
Betty d. Henry & Mary Strickland 23 June
Margaret d. John & Ann Haskele 1 Sep.
John s. John & Ann Gerrard 1 Dec.
Mary d. George & Mary Northover 3 Dec.
George s. Elias & Betty Read 26 Dec.

1766.

Elizabeth d. Thos. & Judith Trubridge 2 Feb.

George s. Raynold & Hannah Randole 6 April
Sarah d. Raynold & Hannah Randole 6 April
James s. John & Mary Stevens 4 May
Henry s. Henry & Jane King 18 May
Jane d. Wm & Martha Humby 19 May
Betty d. Henry & Mary Newman 19 May
Jane d. Wm & Elizabeth Shepherd 25 May
Sarah d. John & Jane Burton 25 May
John s. John & Elizabeth Johnson 11 June
Mary d. Stephen & Mary Smith 15 June
Nancy d. Charles & Hannah Smith 5 Oct.
Wm s. Henry & Elizabeth Penny 2 Nov.
Henry s. Wm & Robina Penny 2 Nov.
Jane d. Wm & Mary King 25 Dec.
John s. Wm & Sarah Powell 26 Dec.

1767.

Mary d. John & Elizabeth Gould 6 Feb.
Elizabeth d. Thos. & Elizabeth Foyle 14 Feb.
John & David ss. Henry & Martha Penny 4 March
Sarah d. Henry & Martha Penny 4 March
Nancy d. John & Mary Pinn 5 April
David Lawes base born 5 April
George s. Thos. & Bridget Coxs 12 April
George s. George & Mary Northover 17 April
Robert & John ss. John & Jane Pigot 19 July
Wm s. Thos. & Alice Turner 26 July
Jane d. Thos. & Judith Trubridge 6 Sep.
Mary d. Wm & Sarah Lush 4 Oct.
Catharine d. Wm & Elizabeth Shepherd 22 Nov.

1768.

Ann d. Wm Vitredge & Jane Russel base-born 31 Jan.
George s. Elias & Elizabeth Read 18 June
Betty d. George Turner & Joyce Belen base born 25 June
James s. Charles & Hannah Smith 17 July
Jane d. John & Mary Stevens 17 July
Edmund s. John & Frances Jolliffe 23 Oct.
Henry s. Wm & Mary King 25 Dec.

1769.

Etty d. Elias & Ann Ingram 11 Jan.
Rhoda d. Harry & Jane King 19 Feb.
Elizabeth d. Samuel and Jane Parrot 19 Feb.
Mary d. John & Mary Bennet 19 March
James s. Thos. & Eliz. Emm 14 May
George s. Thos. & Eliz. Emm 14 May

Sarah d. Francis & Jane Lucas 14 May
John Penny (of riper years) 4 Dec.
Wm Penny (of riper years) 26 Dec.
John Millenor (of riper years) 26 Dec.
Luce Penny 26 Dec.

1770.

Ann d. Charles & Ann Jeffery 7 Jan.
John s. Thos. & Alice Turner 18 Feb.
Mary d. Sam. & Jane Parrot 27 May
W^m s. Henry & Martha Penny 4 June
Betty d. Love & Betty Bungy 4 June
John s. base born John & Mary Penny 22 Oct.
Mary d. base born James Davis & Ann Jollif 27 Oct.
John s. Luke & Susanna Frances 11 Nov.
James s. John & Fanny Jolliffe 9 Dec.
Jane d. W^m & Mary Foyle 25 Dec.

1771.

Henry s. W^m & Sarah Powel 3 Feb.
Luce d. (base born) Timothy Harris & Luce Pin 3 Feb.
W^m s. W^m & Mary Langtry 17 Feb.
Henry s. Henry & Eliz. Penny 6 March
John s. Joseph & Mary Perry 10 March
Joseph s. Thos. & Judith Trowbridge 7 April
W^m s. John & Mary Stephens 27 April
Mary d. Charles & Hannah Smith 28 April
Elias s. George & Mary Ingram 15 May
Ann d. W^m & Mary King 15 May
Stephen (base born) s. Stephen Jay & Mary Cavil 26 May
Hannah d. Reynold & Hannah Randol 11 Aug.
Mary d. John & Ann Woodlands 15 Dec.
Mary d. Francis & Jane Lucas 25 Dec.

1772.

Mary d. Joseph & Mary Witt 5 Jan.
Harry s. David & Ann Gerrard 12 Jan.
John s. John & Mary Bennett 19 Jan.
George s. John & Frances Jolliffe 23 Feb.
Elias s. Elias & Ann Ingram 26 April
W^m s. Love & Betty Bungey 7 June
James s. W^m & Mary Foyle 7 June
John base born s. John & Mary Penny 14 June
Robt s. James & Sarah Feltham 19 July
James s. W^m & Mary Langtry 13 Sep.
John s. W^m & Eliz. Gasper 1 Nov.
Ann d. John & Mary Martin 1 Nov.
Mary d. Robt & Sarah Perry 8 Nov.
Mary d. Joel & Ann Rowden 28 Dec.

1773.

Elizabeth d. John & Mary Chant 17 Jan.
John s. Joshua & Frances Dixon 25 Jan.
John s. Ambrose & Betty Loder 31 Jan.
Mary d. John & Lucy Morris 7 March
John s. William & Elizabeth Cave 17 March
John s. John & Jane Burton 28 March
Samuel s. Samuel & Jane Parret 4 April
John s. John & Mary Pinn 4 April
John s. John & Ann West 14 June
W^m s. Thomas & Betty Gosney 5 Sep.
Mary d. William & Hannah Hewlet 12 Sep.
Sarah d. William & Mary King 17 Oct.
Joseph s. Joseph & Mary Perry 24 Oct.
Thomas s. John & Mary Witt 24 Nov.
Sarah d. Charles & Mary Read 1 Dec.
William s. Francis & Jane Luke 26 Dec.
Luke s. Luke & Susan Francis 26 Dec.

1774.

Elizabeth d. Stephen & Sarah Jay 23 Jan.
John s. Robert & Betty Golden 27 Feb.
John s. John & Betty Francis 27 March
John s. Elias & Anne Ingram 3 April
Thomas s. William & Mary Langtry 24 April
William s. Robert & Sarah Perry 24 April
William s. Joseph & Mary Witt 11 May
Michael s. Thomas & Bridget Cox 29 May
Jane d. James & Sarah Feltham 10 July
Aley d. John & Mary Chant 10 July
William s. John & Fanney Jolliff 17 July
Sarah d. John & Anne Jered 24 July
Charlote d. George & Mary Pinckney 10 Aug.
Elizabeth d. Samuel & Jane Parrot 2 Oct.
William s. William & Mary Foyle 30 Oct.
Jane d. William & Anne Chubb 25 Dec.

1775.

Jacob s. George & Mary Ingram 9 Jan.
Keriah d. William & Elizabeth Peny 9 Jan.
Jemimah d. Thos. & Briget Cox 5 Feb.
John s. Joseph & Fanny Pool 19 Feb.
Fanny d. James Laws & Anne Pool 19 Feb.
Elizabeth d. John & Mary Benet 21 May
Dinah d. Benet & Hanah Read 21 May
Catherine d. Joel & Ann Rowden 5 June
John s. William & Joan Ingram 11 June
James s. William King & Joic Bealon 11 June
Anne d. James & Sarah Feltham 8 Dec.
Henry s. Love & Betty Bungy 25 Dec.

1776.

Jane d. James Smart & Bety Mills 21 Jan.
James s. John & Anne West 24 Jan.
James s. Thomas & Alce Turner 11 March
Lizy d. Joseph & Mary Witte 1 April
John s. John & Betty Smith 10 April
Mary d. William & Anne Chub 15 April
Henry s. William & Mary Laws, Bower
 Chalk, 29 May
Elizabeth d. Francis & Jane Luke 2 June
Anne d. George & Rebecca Hulet 7 July
Henry s. William & Mary King 21 July
Mary d. John & Mary Chant 13 Aug.
Job s. Joseph & Mary Penny 20 Oct.
Thomas s. John & Anne Jeret 27 Oct.
Luezar d. W^m & Mary Langtry 3 Nov.
Elizabeth d. Thos. & Briget Cox 22 Dec.
Charlote d. Henry & Jane King 25 Dec.
Millier d. Stephen & Sarah Jay 25 Dec.
Thos. s. Thos. & Elizabeth Stephens 26
 Dec.

1777.

Mary d. Luke & Susanna Francis 19 Jan.
Joel s. Joel & Anne Rowden 3 Feb.
William s. John & Betty Francis 9 March
James s. Samuel & Jane Parret 16 March
John s. James & Anne Dibbon 13 April
Hannah d. John Penny & Sarah Morris
 (bast^d) 25 May
Jonah s. John & Mary Witt 20 June
Benjamin s. Richard & Anne Combs 27
 July
Moses s. Elias & Anne Ingram 16 Aug.
William s. Ambros & Betty Loder 28 Sep.
Rheuben s. Benet & Hannah Read 5 Oct.
Thomas s. John & Mary Johnson 2 Nov.
James s. John & Jane Benet 16 Nov.
Nancy d. Francis & Jane Lucas 25 Dec.
George s. John & Mary Benet 28 Dec.

1778.

George s. George & Mary Coox 11 Jan.
Job s. Stephen & Sarah Jay 15 March
John s. John & Mary Chant 4 April
Mary d. George & Betty Hulet 14 June
Alcy d. John & Anne West 5 Aug.
William s. John & Betty Smith 14 Aug.
George s. John & Lucy Morris 3 Sep.
John s. George & Rebecca Hulet 3 Sep.
Betty d. John Gibbs & Anne Jolloffe
 (base born) 11 Oct.

William s. John & Mary Jay 18 Oct.
Betty d. Joseph & Faney Pool 25 Oct.
Rebecca d. George & Anne Read 13 Dec.
James s. John & Betty Francis 27 Dec.

1779.

Sarah d. Thomas & Elizabeth Stevens 27
 Jan.
Eli s. Joseph & Elizabeth Emm 7 Feb.
James s. Joseph & Mary Perry 4 April
Charlote d. Richd Lush & Sarah Feltham
 (base born) 4 April
William s. Stephen & Elizabeth Barter 11
 April
Stephen s. William & Sarah Powel 26 May
Charlote d. William & Sarah Powel 26 May
Rebecca d. John & Rebecca Golden 6 June
Betty d. Henry & Martha Penny 22 Aug.
Mary d. Henry & Martha Penny 22 Aug.
Mariah d. Henry & Martha Penny 22 Aug.
Deborah d. Henry & Martha Penny 22
 Aug.
Idith d. Richard & Anne Combs 24 Oct.
James s. William & Mary Gartrey 24 Oct.
Mary d. Thomas & Sarah Jay 31 Oct.
Rebecca d. John & Mary Jay 9 Nov.
James s. William & Mary King 25 Nov.
Anne d. Elias & Anne Ingram 2 Dec.

1780.

James s. Robert & Sarah Penny 2 Jan.
Joel s. Joseph & Mary Witt ⎫ Twins
Joseph s. Joseph & Mary Witt ⎬ 13 Feb.
George s. George & Sarah King 12 March
George s. George & Betty Hulet 26 March
James s. John & Mary Chant 14 May
James s. Joseph & Mary Perry 18 June
Mary d. William Cook & Betty Cox (base-
 born) 25 June
Rose d. Ambros & Betty Loder 25 June
Thomas s. Thos. Parsons & Mary Dowland
 16 July
Rebecca d. William & Mary Jay 23 July
Betty d. John & Mary Penny 3 Sep.
Jenny d. William & Mary Langtry 3 Sep.
Rheuben s. Bennet & Hannah Read 24
 Sep.
James s. Thos. & Sarah Francis 28 Sep.
Betty d. William & Anne Feltham 22 Oct.
Prisilla d. Joseph & Elizabeth Emm 26 Oct.
Mary d. Jeremiah Dowland & Betty Penny
 (base born) 3 Dec.
William s. Joel & Anne Rowden 27 Dec.

BURIALS.

Registrum de Sepultis a septimo die mensis Octobris in Anno D'ni 1552.

Phillip Appary 7 Oct.
Mary King 31 Sep.*
Jone Savidge 31 Sep.
Dorothy Holmes 14 Nov.

1556.

John Darke 22 Aug.
Margaret Cooke 23 Aug.
Margaret Amy vid. 15 Oct.
John Staple 18 Nov.
Wm Turner 18 Feb.
John Streete 22 Feb.
Avice Bryne 10 March

1557.

Julyan Selwood 15 April
Nicholas Davis 19 July
Thomas Skinner 14 June
Ralphe Skinner 19 July
Wm Amis 1 Aug.
Thomas Cooke 19 Sep.
Ellen Wisedome 20 Sep.
Jone Shergall 22 Sep.
Dorothie Newman 28 Sep.
Augustine Pip 1 Oct.
George Marshe 3 Oct.
Mary Bryne 4 Oct.
Olive Good 10 Oct.
Richard Odber 23 Oct.
Margerie Lawse vid. 15 Nov.
Agnes Bennet 15 Nov.
Stephen Wisedome 21 Nov.

1558.

John Still 1 Jan.
Margaret Modull vid. 4 Jan.
James Witt 24 Jan.
Henrie Witt 7 Feb.
Christian Penne 17 March
Alex. Good 7 April
John Brine 17 May
Elizabeth Skinner 19 June
Henry Symmes 27 July
John Lone 19 Aug.

* Entered thus in Register: no means of knowing to which year between 1552 and 1556.

C. G. M.

Elizabeth Dew 25 Aug.
Thomas Penruddocke 5 Sep.
John Elmes 9 Sep.
ffriseweed Savidge 26 Sep.
Wm Savidge 27 Sep.
Marian Gray vid. 14 Oct.
Julyan Olyver 24 Oct.
Elizabeth Harding 26 Oct.
Wm Marsh 27 Oct.
Marie Savidge 5 Nov.
Jone Baslee 5 Nov.
John Olyver 29 Nov.
Alce Curtes & Elizabeth her daughter 11 Dec.

1559.

Wm Poore 8 Feb.
Julyan Danet 9 Feb.
Wm Bayne 27 Feb.
Nicholas Rendall 28 Feb.
Thomas Rendall 2 March
Elizabeth Yellow 8 March
Jone Hink 9 March
John Tempat 14 March
Henrie Danit 27 March
Wm Rendall 28 March
Wm Strong 28 March
Margaret Penny 31 March
Wm Savidge 4 April
John Stroug 4 April
Blase Shergall 4 April
Ellen Harding 29 April
Thomas Shergall 1 May
Nicholas Stayner 2 May
Wm Shergall 2 May
Jone Pip 30 May
Edward Evered 12 July
Stephen fish 14 July
Wm Kenchenton 4 Sep.

1562.

Wm Barron 13 April
Jone Cane 6 July
Agnes Townsend 16 Aug.
Jane Miller 20 Nov.
Wm New 9 Jan.
Roger King 15 Jan.

Mary Wallis 6 Feb.
John Wallis 7 Feb.
John King 18 Feb.
Thomas Harris 16 March
Isabell Streete 6 April

1563.
Jone Woodlocke 13 May
Jone Bryne 21 May
Thomas Lawse 1 Aug.
Robert Savidge 21 Aug.
John Staple 22 Aug.
Ellen Gregorie 14 Oct.
Edith Brine 24 Dec.
Jone King 15 Feb.

1564.
Mary Deane 27 Sep.
Elizabeth Woodlocke 4 Oct.

1565.
Henry Rendall 12 Feb.
John Netton 19 Feb.
Katherine Olyver 20 Feb.
John King 13 May
Cicelye Bryne 23 May

1566.
Stephen Wisedome 25 Dec.

1567.
Nicholas Purnell 26 June
John Cooke 3 Aug.
Alce Squire 25 Dec.
Mary North 1 Aug.
Edith Penne 19 Aug.
Ralphe Streete 20 Aug.
Edith Pip 19 Sep.
Thomas Smith 30 Dec.
Alce Bacon 27 Feb.

1568.
Jone King 29 April
Julyan King 6 May
Agnes Savidge 10 Nov.
Wᵐ Ogborne 16 Dec.

1569.
John Odber 9 Aug.
Anne Patlery 23 Sep.
John Wallis 19 Dec.
Margerie Collins 8 Feb.
Thomas Gilbert 23 Dec.

1571.
Margaret Rendall 2 April
Margaret Gregorie 25 July
Eliner Deane 15 Aug.

1572.
Gilbert Drake 7 Jan.
Robᵗ Prestwood 3 Sep.
Elizabeth Savidge 3 Sep.
John Dew 22 Oct.
Christian Netton 27 Oct.
Olive Vanner 30 Dec.

1573.
Margaret New 5 Sep.
Annis Savidge 30 March
Richard Hill 21 May
John Willis 12 Oct.

1574.
John Dew 30 Jan.
Avice Elmes 7 April
Henry Odber 30 April
Anne Dew 7 July
Richard Lawse (?) 7 Sep.
Leonard Parsons (?) 20 Jan.
Alce .... 22 Feb.
Wᵐ Dew 2 March

1575.
Wᵐ Gay 23 April
Anthony Drake 20 June
Thomas Brine 10 Nov.

1576.
Agnes Brine 24 May
Agnes Harvy 25 June
Thomas Selwood 15 Aug.
Thomas Goodenow 14 Sep.

1577.
Amy Martin 1 March
Jone Netton 6 April
Julyan Baker 15 April

1578.
Luce Lawse 20 March
John Lawse 11 April
Alce Penne 21 April
Mʳ Edward Sainctlowe 6 May

1580.
Thomas Gilbert 24 April
Robert Everly 12 May
Elizabeth Angod 28 June
Thomas Shergall 14 Oct.
John Newman 8 Dec.
Mary King 8 Feb.
Edith Shergall 16 Feb.

1581.
Katherine Due 7 June
Agnes Deane 24 Aug.

Wm Wyat 13 Sep.
John Symmons 12 Feb.
Olive Holmes 13 Feb.

1582.

Richard Humber 30 May.
Margery Rendall 21 June
Richard Humber 16 Dec.
John Olyver 17 Dec.
Joan Wyat 18 Dec.
Avice Streete 22 Dec.
Michaell Netton 25 Dec.
fortune Hunt 28 Feb.
Robert Penruddocke 7 March

1583.

John Cane 1 April
Thomas Bryne 6 April
Johannes Sherman Clericus 8 April
John Cooke 30 May
Thomas King 8 Oct.
Nic'las Savidge 18 Feb.

1584.

Alce Brine 24 April
John Selbye 4 May
Mary Small 14 May
John Deane 26 Aug.
John Good 19 March

1585.

Thomas Rendall 9 April
John Savidg 23 June
Mary Prow 25 June
John Pope 19 Jan.

1586.

Jone Rendall 4 April
Thomas Elmes 17 April
Ralph Netton 3 June
Tho. Jeffery 10 June
Alce Rendall 4 July
Dorithy (?) Savidg 16 July
Margaret Strete 21 July
Jone Stroug 21 Sep.
Thomas Angod 2 Dec.
John Rendall 5 Dec.

1587.

Jane Lawse 26 May
Sibell Penny 27 May
Alce Langtree 7 June
Thomas Due 17 June
Friseweed Okeford 19 June
Joane Newman 21 Aug.
Thomas King 30 Aug.
Thomas Savidge 2 Dec.
Michaell Selwood 12 Dec.

Annis Angod 20 Dec.
Grace King 28 Jan.
Nicholas Rendall 2 March
Jane Angod 12 March

1588.

Agnes Golde 8 April
Thomas Rendall 6 May
Thomas Whitmarsh de fiefield 2 June
Julyan Strete 13 July
Christobell Savidge 2 Aug.
Mary Scudd 6 Aug.
Anne Curtes 9 Aug.
John Lodge 2 Jan.
Joane Plowman 19 Feb.

1589.

Edith Plowman 31 March
Thomas Okeford 3 July
Jane Pitchland 8 Nov.
Katherine Angod 19 Nov.

1590.

Alex. Strete 28 May
Agnes Good 22 Aug.
Thomas Selby 3 Nov.
Jone Scammell 15 Dec.
John Brine 20 Jan.

1592.

Walt. Savidg 31 May
Richard North 7 June
Agnes Ayers 13 July
Jone Newman 21 Aug.
Thomas Brine 15 Sep.
Jone flower 6 Oct.
Phillis New 5 Nov.
Thomas Newman 28 Nov.
Jone Lodg 3 Dec.
Wm Savidge 27 Dec.
Jane Selwood 14 Jan.
John Pitchland 23 Jan.
Joyce Penruddocke 31 Jan.

1593.

Avice fishe 2 May
John Rendall 6 May
Dorothie Poten mortem obiit 20 May
Christian Lawse 14 June
. . . . Okeford 20 June
Margaret Sainctlow 24 Aug.
John Newman 2 Sep.
Thomas Browne gener. 25 Jan.
Mary Bennet 26 Aug.
Thomas New 16 Dec.
Julian Bryne 6 Jan.

1594.

Walter Follyat 11 April
Sir John de Fiefield 19 April

Henricus Miller 28 Nov.

1595.

Edith Rendall 12 Jan.
Elizabeth Penny 12 Jan.
Jone Mountague 29 Jan.
John Mountague 12 Feb.
Thomas King 28 April
Elizabeth King 12 May
Arthur Golding 6 June
Stephen Edney 28 Sep.
John Marshman 14 Feb.
Alce Laurence 25 Feb.
Avice Curtes 10 March
Jone Cooke vid. 15 March

1596.

Agnes Antramme 12 April
Alce Gilbert 1 May
John Harris 4 Aug.
Wm Cleydon 22 Aug.
Priscilla Whitmarsh 28 Nov.
John Good 17 Jan.
Margaret Plowman 29 Jan.
Luce Wilkins 4 Feb.

1597.

Ralphe Skinner 11 April
Joane Penny 30 April
Guilielmus Brine 1 May
Rodolphus Elmes 14 June
Henricus Garland 10 Aug.
Anna Smith 31 Aug.
Johannes Pillin 6 Sep.
ffranny Brine 16 Sep.
Maria Ledford 21 Sep.
Walterus Angod 22 Sep.
Thomas Lodge 26 Sep.
Arthurus King 13 Nov.
Elizabeth Bryne 14 Nov.
Anna Sainctlow fil. Johannis gener. 2 Dec.
Vid. Seynens 23 Dec.

1598.

Joanna Knight 15 Feb.
Maria Cane 22 Feb.
Vid. Knight 22 Feb.
Jacobus Cooke 23 Feb.
Guilielmus Savidge 28 Feb.
Dorothea Symmes 22 March
Alicia Evered 24 March
Henricus Everet 9 April
Johannes Clytherlie 10 April
Stephanus Langtree 13 April
Egidius Ledford 16 April
Amy Penny 19 April
Johannes Ledford 19 April

Joanna Witt 21 April
. . . . Bryne (?) 21 April
Thomas Dier 2 May
Johannes Rendall 14 May
Bartholomeus King 22 May
Johannes Due 24 May
Agnes Rendall 31 May
Thomas Brine 2 June
Alicia Miller 12 June
Avicia Symmes 9 July
Thomas Loxely 27 July
Margareta Warnmm 6 Aug.
Johannes Sellwood 22 Nov.
Vidua Butler 28 Dec.

1599.

Avicia Rendall 3 Jan.
Gabriel King 2 March
Maria Pennie 5 April
Georgius Clytherlie 6 May
Thomas Kinge 29 Sep.
Alicia Whitmarsh 11 Feb.

1600.

Johannes Cane 14 Oct.
Georgius Aynold 5 Nov.
Petrus Stone 21 Nov.

1601.

Maude Harney 9 Feb.
Henry Penny 2 April
William Jaye s. of William Jaye 22 April
John Savaige 28 June
Elizabeth Smale d. William 3 July
Anna Neweman vid. 25 July
Gyles Man widow 9 Jan.
Peter fflecher 22 Jan.
John Simes 16 Feb.
Aymie Angod vidua 7 March
. . . . Savage 7 March
Catharin Ault

1602.

Joane Davis d. Henry Davis 8 July
Grace Cooke d. John Cooke 8 July
John Cane s. Robert Cane 18 Sep.
Mary Savidge d. William 14 Oct.
Annis Skinner 11 Dec.
John Scammell 23 March

1603.

William Penny of Stoake 27 March
John Savidge of Stoake 29 Sep.
Robert Holly s. Thomas Holly 12 Oct.
Joane Leonard 17 Nov.
John Streete 10 Jan.
Alexander Randoll the younger 21 Jan.
Thomas Deane 25 Jan.

Ellinore Witt 4 Feb.
Widdow Lanctry 12 Feb.
Phillip Clie s. Simon Clie 25 Feb.
Phillis White wife of Ralphe White 26 Feb.
Alexander Bell 14 Mar.

1604.

Joane Brine w. Thomas Brine 29 May
Joane Whitemarshe w. Thomas Whitemarshe 4 Feb.
Thomas Streete 20 Feb.

1605.

Michaell Angod 3 April
Henry Good 24 Aug.
William Gilbert 8 Nov.
Isabell Gilbert 25 Nov.
William Scammell 5 Dec.
Thomas Witte 21 Dec.
Edward Witt s. Thomas Witt the younger 9 Jan.
Alexander Street s. Jane Street widdow 10 Mar.

1606.

Edgar Thringe 20 April
Elizabeth Lodge of Easte Gerardstone, widdow, 23 May
Jane Lawes d. John Lawes 16 May
John ffrances 25 May
Alice ffrances 29 May
Elizabeth Bateman 20 July
Edmonde Deane s. Daniell Deane 3 Aug.
Mr ffowke Drake, parson of Fyfeilde 7 Aug.
William Skinner 12 Aug.
Thomas Angod 14 Aug.
Hughe Randoll s. John Randoll of Stoake 22 Jan.
Annis Thringe d. Edgar Thringe 3 March
Thomas Kinge of Stoake 13 March
Ralphe Good 22 March

1607.

Thomas Phrippe s. John Phripp 2 April
Alice Brooke w. John Brooke 12 April
Edmond Beerhe(?) 29 April
Annis Dawne 26 April
Steeven Odber 1 May
Avis Speeringe of* William Speeringe 8 July
Elizabeth Phripp widdow 5 Sep.
Melior Haviland d. Mr Thomas Haviland 24 Dec.
Elizabeth Penn of* Henry Penn 11 Feb.

* Sic.

Ellinor Randoll d. John Randoll of Knighton 2 March
Bartholomew Goode 4 March

1608.

Joane Whitmarshe w. William Whitmarshe of West Gerardstone 28 Mar.
John Newman 2 April
Thomas Witt s. James Witt 16 April
Alice Lawes w. John Lawes the elder 21 April
Brigett Pillon d. John Pillon 2 June
Mary Good wyddow 31 July
Elizabeth Gregory 27 Oct.
Thomas Streete the elder 18 Nov.
Beniamin Drake 15 Dec.
William Penruddocke s. Sir Tho. Penruddocke 18 Dec.

1609.

Margerett Chubb 28 March
Alexander Randoll senr. 1 May
Maude Savidge d. William Savidge 22 July
Edward Kinge s. Christopher Kinge 24 July
Ralphe White 6 Aug.
Denize Savidge w. William Savidge 17 Aug.
Joane Streete wyddow 8 Sep.
John Goode 15 Oct.
Walter Holly s. Thomas Holly 15 Oct.
Joane Newe 30 Nov.
Mawde ffrances 27 Jan.
Ralphe Clenton 11 Feb.
Elizabeth Golden 25 Feb.
James Creede s. William Creede 16 Mar.
Anne Pounce d. Wm Pounce 17 Mar.

1610.

Thomas Deane s. Daniell Deane 16 April
John Witt s. Thomas Witt 28 April
Leah Oliver d. William Oliver 4 May
William Thomas 4 May
John Collins 22 June
Millisant ffrancis 23 June
Jane Rendoll 6 July
Edward Warde 10 Oct.
Jane Rendoll 26 Nov.
Thomas Rendoll 7 Nov.
Joane Lambe (?) 5 Jan.
Agnes Good 14 Jan.
Marye Moxam 14 Jan.
Thomas Shergoll 2 Feb.
Elizabeth Monday 10 Feb.
Edward Kinge s. Thomas Kinge 24 Feb.
Richard Whittier 9 March

1611.

John Rendoll of the greene 29 March
John Wilkins s. John Wilkins 6 April
Margery Mudford 6 April
Henry Griffithe s. John Griffithe 12 April
Ralf Segare 12 April
Mary ffrancis 15 April
John Stedmun 17 April
Marye Angod w. William Angod 14 June
Margery Browne vid. 20 June
Thom. Rendoll 21 June
Katherine Kinge 17 Aug.
Sibill Peny 19 Sep.
Martha Stedmun d. Jhs. Stedmun 5 Nov.
George Teynt 6 Nov.

1612.

Joane Griffine d. John Griffine 28 March
Amye Griffine w. John Griffine 2 May
Stephen Cook 3 May
William Willoughby 29 May
Margret Kinge 5 June
Moses Newman 6 June
Agnes Savadge wydow 11 June
Jane Shergoll d. Thomas Shergoll 19 July
Avis Garland 22 Sep.
Alce Kinge 25 Oct.
Marye Miller 12 Nov.
Martha Sayntloe 28 Jan.
Harry Odburre 6 March

1613.

Katherine King 17 May
Thomas Angod 29 May
Watkin Gruffin 20 June
Robt. Tillier 23 June
John Peny of Stoake the elder 5 Aug.
John Wilkins 10 Sep.
Joane Miles 30 Oct.
Nicholas Clinton 17 Nov.
Joane Streete 5 Dec.
Judith Skeele w. Richard 11 Dec.

1614.

Daniell Deane 30 March
John Lawes the elder 1 May
Alexander Curteise 12 May
Agnes Wiatt 29 May
Michaell Streete 10 Oct.
Edward King 5 March
Katherin Streete 7 March

1615.

Dominicke spur. Joannis Street 9 May
Agnes w. Clement White 20 May
Isabell w. Ralph Whitmarsh 31 July
Mary d. Thomas Witte 14 Sep.

Cicilly w. William Whitmarsh 3 Oct.
Agnes w. Raph Miles 10 Dec.
Margret Miles 17 Dec.
Priscilla Pillen 29 Dec.
Alexander ffrancis 26 Dec.
Alice Witt 6 Jan.
Ellinore Penie 25 Jan.
John Jey 25 Jan.
Rachell Harvie 27 Jan.
Jane Hollye 4 Feb.
Bartholomew Peny senior 5 Feb.
Sible Savery d. Willm 24 Feb.

1616.

Dorothie Antram 23 June
Margerie Whitmersh 24 Aug.
John Hurny 7 Dec.
Agnes Cooke 27 Dec.
Joane widdow of Willm Peny 10 March

1617.

Elizabeth Whitemarsh 3 Aug.
Olive King 29 Sep.
Solomon King 26 Dec.
Elizabeth White widowe 1 Feb.

1618.

Marie King widowe 25 March
Edith Cooke widowe 17 April
Thomas Whitmarshe 18 April
Henry Penny 31 July
Mr. John Saintlo gentleman 26 Oct.
Thomas s. Mr Adam Waters clark 12 Dec.
Elizabeth w. Mr. William Grove of Gerrardstone — Dec.
Steven Savidge 20 Dec.
William Scammell 20 Dec.
Robert Cane 21 Jan.
Edith Marshman widow 6 Feb.

1619.

William Goldstone 19 April
Thomas Brine the yonger of Stoake 20 Aug.
Marian Streete widdowe 23 Sep.
Jane Newe widdowe 5 Jan.
Willm s. Edward Foxhanger 18 Jan.
John Griffin 9 Feb.

1620.

Joane Hodder 2 April
Agnes d. George Scammell 5 May
Alice w. Willm Bull 8 May
Thomas s. Timothie Lodge 8 June
Thomas Brine the elder of Stoake 26 June
Michael d. John Penny of Mountsorrell 22 July

Joane w. John Pillen 29 July
Henry s. Henry Scud *alias* Gilbert 29 Aug.
Julian White 14 March
Anne w. Mr. Willm. Grove junior 17
    March
Katherine Acklin 18 March

1621.

Margaret w. Edmond White 28 May
Thomas Whitemarsh 2 July
Alexander King 24 Oct.
William s. Henry Norris 22 Nov.
Elizabeth Smalwell widdow 22 Nov.
Thomas s. Henry Scud *alias* Gilbert 28
    Nov.
Bridget w. Alexander ffrancis 28 Nov.
Thomas s. Henry Scud *alias* Gilbert 1
    Feb.

1622.

Dennis w. Nicolas Whitmarsh 25 March
Amy d. John Griffin 30 March
Alice spur. of Elinor Lylly 20 April
Elizabeth Randall w. Jo. Randall 7 Oct.
Joan North vid. 10 June
Henry Angood w. An. Angood 10 June
Jo. Aires 20 Dec.
Jo. Paradise 6 Jan.
Tho. Witt 19 Feb.

1623.

William Hardiman 3 Nov.
Ralphe Whitemarsh 11 Dec.
Joan Randall 12 Dec.
Elizabeth Angood 16 Jan.
Francis Ernely 14 Feb.
William Michel 2 Feb.

1624.

Joan Dean 16 April
Thomas King 21 April
Agnes d. John Griffin 28 April
Agnes Skiner 8 May
John Ploman 30 May
Yedith Good 20 Oct.
John Moxam 5 Nov.
Elizabeth d. Alexander frances 28 Nov.
Yedeth Simes 2 Dec.
John Lodge 19 Dec.
Jone w. John Hale 14 Feb.

1625.

Bartholomu King of Stoke, s. Bartholomu
    King 15 June
Thomas Cope s. frances Cope 14 Aug.
John Harrod s. Thomas Harrod of Sales-
    bury 9 Nov.

? ? 5 Dec.
? Bryne of Stoke 20 Feb.
Christian Bartrume w. of Thomas Bar-
    trum 3 March

1626.

Tomson Foxhanger w. Robert 4 May
Agnes Savadge d. William Savadge 24
    June
Thomas Rendoll 22 July
An King w. Bartholomu King 18 Oct.
Mestres Margret w. Master Anthoney
    Browne 1 Nov.
Barthollmu Penney of Stoke Verden 15
    Nov.
Nicholas Whitmarsh of Stoke 30 Dec.

1627.

Grace Harvey w. John Harvey of Stoke
    7 April
William Savage of Stoke 15 May
Thomas Dyer 24 May
Catherine Brine w. Thomas Brine 18
    Oct.
Honour Hancock w. Th. Hancock 24
    Oct.
Elizabeth Holland d. Thomas Holland 8
    Nov.

1628.

Lucy Randoll d. Alxdr. 31 March
Thomas Randoll s. Alxdr. 1 April
Thomas Bertram 15 July
Robert Rover 25 July
Sibill Finckly 5 Aug.
Walter Penny s. John Peny 4 Sep.
Henry Shargoll s. Wilkes Shargoll 16
    Nov.
Thomas Dew s. William Dew 20 Jan.
Marie Witt w. James Witt 26 Jan.
Thomas Lylye 18 Feb.
Marye Randole w. John Randole 4 March
Alice Hutcheus vidua 8 March
Margaret Scammell w. George Scammell
    22 March

1629.

Wilyam King 4 May
Anna Odber vid. 6 May
Mr. Walter Waller vicar of Broad Chalk
    14 May
Mrs. Anne Penny w. John Penny 22
    July
John Randall 3 Dec.
Anne Whitmarshe 7 Dec.
Grissill Sims w. Christopher Sims 13 Feb.
Margaret Pennie w. Tho. Pennie 25 Feb.

1630.

Marie Foxe d. Edward Foxe 7 April
John Brocked 10 May
Will. Savadge s. Will. Savadge 24 June
Edward Foxe s. Edward Foxe 18 July
John Golden 18 July
Willm. Hayes 6 Oct.
Jane Molins d. Richard Molins 11 Nov.
Joane Good 16 Nov.
John Randall 8 Dec.
Nicholas bastard child of Joane Lambe
    16 Dec.
Joane King 29 Dec.
The wife of John Nott 12 Jan.
The widdowe Lillie 16 Jan.
Elizabeth Grove w. Willm. the younger
    19 Jan.
John Sims 22 Jan.
Gabriel King s. Thomas 30 Jan.
William Antrum — March

1631.

Eliza: Whitmarsh w. Thomas White-
    marsh 12 April
Robt. Stent — April
Edw. Bennet 26 May
Mary Scudd d. Henry Scudd — May
Margaret Pen 8 Oct.
Thomas Lodg s. Timothie Lodge 9 Dec.
Christopher Sims 15 Dec.
Elizabeth Saintlo 24 Feb.
Katherina Seagar 8 March

1632.

Lewes Randoll 18 May
Alf. Gould 29 May
Walter Savidg 2 June
Henry Penn 20 June
William Grove 21 June
Guliel. Grove s. Tho. Grove 2 Aug.
Jeana Grove wife Tho. Grove 3 Aug.
Dorothea Deane 23 Sep.
John Hare 29 Sep.
Thomas Seagor 10 Oct.
Martha Archer 16 Oct.
France Harwood d. Mr. Harwood de Sa-
    rum nova 13 Dec.
Alecia Evens 2 March
Emm. Stocken 14 March

1633.

Elizabetha Witt 20 March
Georgius Saintloe s. Edwardi Saintloe 1
    June
Ann Penny d. Edmund Penny 29 June
Nickolas Penny 22 Sep.
Elizabetha Brine w. Gualteri Brine 25 Oct.

Margaret Dyer 24 Dec.
Martha King 9 Jan.
Bartholomew Penny 25 Jan.
Mrs. Alice Watkinson 26 Feb.
John Pillion 21 March

1634.

Avice Evens 4 May
John Cooke 30 June
Joan Ledford 8 July
Ann Penny 23 Aug.
George Scammell 9 Sep.
Margaret Randol 20 Sep.
Maria White 2 Nov.
Alexander Frances 8 Dec.
Dorothie Gray 14 Jan.
Ellis Miles 1 March
William Angod 10 March

1635.

Simon Penny 30 March
Dora Jana Grove wife Gulielmi Grove 22
    April
Margaret Savage 19 May
Cecilia Bennet 28 May
Thomas Finckly 1 June
Michael Penny 11 June
Guillielmus Angod 11 July
Mr Johannes Penny 9 Aug.
Ann Davis 30 Aug.
Cecilia Dew 14 Feb.
Thomas Curtis 26 Feb.
Josephus Cooke 16 March

1636.

Maria Archer 23 April
Joane Randol w. John Randol 3 May
Henry Penny s. John Penny 21 June
John Randol s. Henry Randoll 20 July
John Dewe s. Bartholomew Dewe 8 Dec.
Mrs Saintloe wife Mr Lawrence 7 Feb.
Lawrence Sayntloe s. Mr Lawrence 8 Feb.

1637.

Richard Baker 4 May
Tagi Witt 28 May
Anthonie Lydford 1 June
John Savadge 8 Sep.
Thomas Moxam s. Th. Moxam — Sep.
Sara Penny — Sep.
T. Moxam — Oct.
Jane Spering 7 Nov.
Jone Bennet 12 Nov.
Margaret Skinner 1 Dec.
Marie King 14 Dec.
Marie Lodg 21 Dec.
Peregrinus (moriebatur super campo) 31
    Dec.

John Randol 19 Jan.
Joane Sims 28 Jan.
William Good 25 Feb.

1638.

John Deane 25 April
Elizabeth Pen 25 June
Ann Good 18 July
Alice Penny 25 July
Alexander Randol 5 Sep.
Katarin Penny 5 Sep.
Avis Folliat 9 Sep.
John Ford 15 Sep.
John Cooke 22 Sep.
John Folliat 23 Sep.
Annis Lawes 23 Sep.
Ann Cooke 24 Sep.
Mary Davies 1 Oct.
Elizabeth Antram 9 Oct.
Michael Penny 23 Oct.
John Ford 24 Oct.
Edmund Saint Lowe 2 Nov.
Avis Whitemarsh 2 March

1639.

Ann Clouter 6 May
Peregrina puella 23 May
Christopher Ford 16 July
John Randol 14 Oct.
Edith Fulford 20 Oct.
Walter Bryne 24 Oct.
Marie Burt 3 Dec.
Michael Street 25 Dec.

1640.

Michael Penny 25 March
Annis Penny 27 March
Laurence Saintlo s. Mr Laurence Saintlo 6
　April
John Street 23 April
Hester Bennet 1 May
Walter Scud 19 May
Bartholomew Dewe 24 May
Jeane Odburre 11 July
Richard Wheeler 15 July
Roger White 8 Aug.
Joane Bryne 15 Aug.
Mr William Grove 31 Aug.
Ann Pillen 13 Oct.
Mr Anthony Browne 21 Nov.
Mathewe Fulford 1 Dec.
Ann Street 26 Dec.
Avis Whitmarshe 14 Feb.
Alex. Penny 21 March

1641.

Hellen Dewe 12 June

Thomas Bennet 30 June
Christopher Holly 11 Aug.
John Street 5 Sep.
William Short 7 Sep.
Martha King 18 Sep.
George Bacon (?) 24 Oct.
Mr Richard Browne 23 Nov.
Robert Antram 9 Feb.
John Randol 22 Feb.

1642.

Anne Randol 20 April
Thomas Lamb 20 May
Elizabeth Merifeild 26 May
John Sansebury (?) 18 June
Joane Witt 9 July
Grace Edny 16 July
Thomas Page 18 July
Anthony Angod 6 Aug.
Ann Golden 31 Dec.
John Golden 12 Feb.
William Dewe 2 March
Mary Lydford 12 March
Richard Skeele 17 March
Thomas Shergoll 23 March

1643.

Thomas Andrew 4 May
Julian Edney 9 May
Christopher Scammell 14 June
Elizabeth Dewe 15 June
Edward Priest 30 July
Margery Cook 3 Aug.
John Griffin 15 Aug.
Mary Short 18 Sep.
Michael Penny 8 Oct.
Anne Segor 3 Dec.
Mrs Peyton 13 Dec.
Robert Shargale 15 Jan.
Thomas Golding 28 Jan.
Anne Shargale 4 Feb.

1644.

Marie Boulton 1 May
Alice Holmes 28 May
Walter Edney 11 Aug.
John White 15 Aug.
Mr Robert Peyton 23 Aug.
Edmond White 28 Aug.
Anne Miles 1 Sep.
John Penny 6 Sep.
Thomas Francis 8 Sep.
Thomas Dewe 13 Oct.
Francis Holly 15 Nov.
John Dewe 18 Dec.
Robert Whitmarsh 1 Jan.
John White 14 Jan.

Alice Randole 8 Feb.
Mr Edmond Browne 12 Feb.
Avis Wagge 15 Feb.

1645.

John Chubbe 12 April
Katherine Deane 25 April
John s. John Bundy 3 July
William Penne 30 Nov.
Elizabeth Saintloe d. Mr. Laurence Saint-
loe 18 July
Thomas Witte s. Cornelius Witt — Dec.
Anne Witt a widow — Dec.
Mary Norris d. Henry Norris 20 Dec.
Avis widow Folliat 6 Jan.
Margaret w. John King 23 Jan.
William Dewe 25 Jan.
The wife of Anthony Archer 15 March

1646.

Sarah w. John Smallwell 30 March
Ralph Penne 5 April
Anne St Loe d. Mr Laurence St Loe 11
April

1647.

. . . . . Norris w. Hen. Norris 6 May
Christian Chub d. John Chub 9 May
. . . . . Witt 31 July

1648.

Amy Whitmarsh 3 April
Mary Due widdow 7 June
Jone Randol d. Henry Randol 18 June
Ralph Miles 18 June
Catharine Marshman w. John 30 June
Ralph Street 7 Feb.

1649.

Mary Lamb 27 March
Richard Shergol 10 April
Alice Streete 3 July
Thomas Finckly 13 July
John Randol 24 July
Martha Newman 8 Oct.
Susanna Andrews 19 Nov.
Jane Plowman 2 Dec.
John Penn 21 Jan.
Mary Holly 22 Feb.
William Penny s. John 28 March

1650.

Jone Dew wid. 9 April
Bartho. King 16 April
Joyce Odber of William 17 April
Amy Whitmarsh w. William 31 May
Beniamin Stone s. William 2 Aug.
Jane Lawes s. William 10 Aug.
Agnes Shergoll w. Richard 22 Oct.

1651.

Agnes Shergoll w. Robert 12 April
Thom. Randoll s. Tho. 3 July
William Whitmarsh 10 July
William Goode s. Henry 24 Aug.
Margaret Bennett w. Tho. 18 Oct.
Mary Deane d. William 1 Nov.
Willm. Langtrey 3 Jan.

1652.

Henry Good sen^r 30 March
George Moore 30 March
Christian Randoll w. Alex. — April
Walter Newman's wife — May
Bartho. Segar — June
John Lawes 3 Aug.
Thomas Deane 3 Oct.
Anne Miles d. Cornelius 5 Oct.
Maude Penny 7 Feb.
Annis Penny d. Thomas — Feb.
Anne Curtis widow 11 March
Tho. Penny stump* 18 March
Morris Mountygue 20 March

1653.

Thomas Angood 12 April
Richard Aubrey, of Broad Chalke, Esq.,
died at Chalke, 21 of October, and
buried at Kington St. Michael, the
26 of the same month. Anno 1652.
Kington is neare Chippenham in N.
Wilts.

(To this entry the following pencil note
is appended : "Probably the handwriting
of John Aubrey, the Antiquarian.")

(Signed) E. W. AWDRY.

[End of first Register Book.]

1660.†

Mary Penne wife of Ralph 31 Aug.
Nicholas Savidge of Knighton 21 Sep.
Willm. Michell of Stoke 26 Sep.

1661.

Ambrose New 20 June
William Lawes 4 Aug.
Thomas Deane s. Thomas 12 Aug.
John Odber & Thomas Odber ss. of Henry
21 Aug.
Nicholas ffrancis s. Alexander 18 Sep.
Margery Shergoll w. Richard 28 Sep.
Marian Goal 27 Nov.
Grace Osmond wid. 19 Sep.
Samuell King s. Samuell 26 Dec.
Mary Way d. Richard 26 Feb.

* Sic.
† Registers 1653—1660 are missing, but see
Appendix.

1662.

Elizabeth Dew d. Thomas 10 July
Jone Mullens d. Richard 13 Aug.
Ralph Miles s. Isaac 25 Aug.
Elizabeth New w. Thomas 1 Sep.
Elizabeth Randoll w. Thomas of Stoke 11 Oct.
Henry Scud *alias* Guilbert 18 Oct.
Elizabeth Randoll w. Thomas, North Street, 12 Jan.
John freep (?) 19 Jan.
Mary Randoll w. John of Churchstile 20 Feb.

1663.

Ursula Antram w. Robert 11 May
John Smith the miller 27 May
William Odber s. Thomas of Stoke 18 June
William Archer s. William de ... 23 June
* Th. Randoll s. John at Churchstile 21 March
*   wid. wife of Ralph 23 March

1664.

* . . . . s. Nicholas 8 April
* . . . . w. Henry 5 June
* . . . . 11 June
John Scamell 29 July
* . . . . w. John Randoll 4 Sep.
* Willi. . . . 11 Sep.
* Jane . . . w. Nicholas 12 Jan.
* Eliz . . . mm w. Ralph 14 Jan.

1665.

Peter Streat 4 April
Mary Haylocke wid. w.† Robert 22 June
Sibelly Jenkins w. Jenkins 24 Nov.

1666.

Susan Goulding w. John 1 April
John Stocky 18 Aug.
Jane Speering of Stoke w. William 8 Oct.
Edward foxhanger 7 Oct.
Alexander Randoll 24 Dec.
John Deane s. William 3 Jan.
William Savidge of Stoke 8 Jan.
John Sanders of Knighton 24 Jan.
Gartrude Good d. Ralph 18 Feb.
Christopher Cook of Stoke 12 March

1667.

Michaell Huntly 9 May
Michaell ffarrant 26 May
Thomas Dew 25 June

Michaell Best w. John Best & d. Henry Peny 8 July
Avis Michell widow w. William 30 July
William Skinner 22 Nov.
Gabriell King of Stoke 2 Dec.
Elizabeth Penny d. John of Moulshill 5 Dec.
Sara King d. Alexander of London 20 March

1668.

Katherine Lilly w. John 13 April
Mary Aclyn w. George 22 May
Williams Evans s. Roger 1 June
Timothy Lodge s. Timothy 9 June
Thomas Evans s. Roger 11 June
Katherine Storke d. Hen. 24*
Philis Lawes w. John * Aug.
Edward Penny of Stoke * Sep.
Richard North servant to Robert Jeffe ... 5*
.... ria Way w. Richard 22 Jan.
Mary Carter w. William 2 Feb.
Thomas King of Stoke * March
Nicholas Penny de Stoke * March
Timothie Way s. Timothie 24 March

1669.

Thomas Combs of Stoke 23 July
John Penny shephard, s. John of Moulson senr. 19 Sep.
Anna Richards d. Thomas 23 Sep.
Henry Odber 18 Oct.
Cyrill Penny w. Soloman 1 Jan.
Stephen Thorn 23 Jan.

1670.

Cornelius Witt s. Cor. 15 April
Walter Gray 31 May
Mary Pen w. Thomas 2 June
Susan Watkinson w. Henry 8 July
Thomas Penn 21 Aug.
Thomas Batt 3 Sep.
Anthony Burd
Anne Archer w. Will. and widow 10 Sep.
William Odbur 15 Sep.
Samuel Penny 23 Sep.
Henry Davy(?) 15 Oct.
Dorothy Good d. Ralphe Good 8 Nov.
Dorothy Good w. Ralphe Good 23 Nov.
Jone Smith widow 18 Nov.
ffrancis Watkinson d. Henry 28 Nov.
John Penny de Moulshall 12 Dec.
Robert Scammell 14 Feb.
Jane Randol w. Anthony 17 Feb.
Edith Segar w. Will. Segar 16 March

* Destroyed by mice.   † Sic.

* Destroyed by mice.

1671.

Will. Nashe s. Giles 15 June
Emme Whit widdow 8 Aug.
W* . . . enny s. John 13 Aug.
* . . . Good d. Ralphe 31 Aug.
* . . . Deane 1 Oct.
* . . . awes s. Thomas Dawes of
 Sarum 19 Nov.
* . . . Sloper d. John Sloper, vicar,
 17 Nov.
* . . d. 16 Dec.
* . . eete d. Ralph 17 Dec.
* . . . Ackland d. George 20 Nov.
K* . . hite d. Henry 2 March

1672.

A* . . wes d. William 12 Jan.†
K* . . . e White d. Henry 7 March†
Mary White d. Henry 13 April
Bartholomew Penny 5 June
Jane Thorne wid. 13 June
Elizabeth Lawes d. William 13 July
Edward Bidlecom 14 July
John King 17 Sep.
William Lawes 7 Nov.

1673.

Mary Bennet w. Thomas 1 April
Elenor Miles w. Isaak 23 April
Avis Batt d. Thomas 21 May
Mary Lawes d. John 25 May
Thomas Newby s. Henry 8 June
Jane Nichols a Base 9 June
Thomas Bennet 27 June
Jane Nott d. Nicholas 28 June
Joseph Haiter a Base 2 July
William Shergol s. Richard 10 Aug.
Jane Randol d. Tho. Ran. 13 Nov.
Ann Tapper w. John 17 Dec.

Christable Norris w. Hen. 14 Jan.
Elizabeth Harvy w. Edward 9 Feb.

1674.

Ursula ffripp widd 10 May
George Lawes s. John 8 July
Mary Miles d. Cornelius 23 July
George Lawes s. George 19 Aug.
Editha Penny w. William 20 Oct.
John Randol (Smith) 4 Nov.
Widow Bennet 18 Feb.
William Randol s. Antho. 10 March
Sarah Streete 14 March

1675.

Phillis Streete 24 June
John Lilly 12 July
Henry Randol 11 Nov.
Edward Brine 12 Dec.
Mihill Moxam 18 Jan.
Alce Randol 22 Jan.
Richard Moulins 22 Feb.
Mary Deare 29 Feb.

1676.

Ann Penny, Wid. 29 March
John Marchant s. Will. ——
Thomas New 2 June
Jane Savage d. Nicho. 14 May
George Randol 20 May
Alece Angod 3 July
Richard Wag 1 Nov.
Sarah Biggs d. Will. 20 Nov.
Thomas Reade 21 Feb.

1678.

John Miles 2 July*
Rich. Shergol 27 July*

A REGISTER OF ALL SUCH BURIALS WHICH HAVE BEEN MADE OF BROAD-CHALK IN THE COUNTY OF WILTS SINCE THE FIRST AUGUST 1678 ACCORDING TO AN ACT THEN MADE FOR BURYING IN WOOLLEN.

1677.

Ursely Lawes w. George Lawes 25 Sep.
Susanna Andrewes d. Will. Andrewes 27
 Sep.
Alexander ffrances 1 Oct.
Jane ffox wid. 31 Oct.
Ann Penny wid. 30 Nov.
Margaret Evans w. Tho. Evans 28 Dec.

* Destroyed by mice.
† So entered in Register.

Ann Smith w. Christo. Smith 31 Dec.
Joseph Rose, base, 8 Jan.
John ffoliat 16 March

1678.

Thomas Randol s. John 25 March
Thomas Vane a stranger 2 June

* These entries for 1678 are thus arranged in
the Register, and none appear in 1677; but the
next Register begins in 1677, and is headed as
above.

Katharine Bigs d. Sarah Bigs 28 June
Abigaile Angod w. Anthony 28 July
John ffisher s. Thom. ffisher 24 Aug.
Henry Hicks 14 Oct.
Edmund Harvy s. Edm. 16 Oct.
Will. Harford's child still borne 1 Nov.
Will. s. Joane Combs, Base. 2 Nov.
The son of Nicho. Savadge still borne 1 Nov.
Jone Priest 5 Jan.
John ffrancis 8 Jan.
Tho. Westbury 30 Jan.
Jean White 30 Jan.
Elizabeth Pitman 2 March

1679.

. . . (illegible) 15 June
Anthony Archer 1 July
John Randol 7 Aug.
Ann Penny 14 Aug.
Grace Penny 28 Dec.
Avis White w. Henry 31 Dec.
John Penny of Stoke 22 Jan.
Joane King 25 Jan.
Margaret Scammel 18 Feb.
George Read 22 Feb.
Margaret Brine 23 Feb.
Andrew Deane 8 Feb.
Ann Evans 3 March
Sarah Bundy 10 March
Ann Witmarsh 21 March

1680.

Will. Hutchins 26 March
Katharine Penny 14 April

1681.

John Streete 6 May
Ralph Streete 28 June
Mary King 20 July
Walter Whitmarsh 4 Aug.
Timothy Lodge 8 Aug.
Thomas Aubery 19 Aug.
Mary Moulins 23 Sep.
Cornelius Witt 27 Sep.
Christopher Penny 27 Sep.
Henry Deane 11 Oct.
Alice Davis 12 Oct.
Jane Lawes 15 Oct.
Sarah Baker 20 Oct.
Henry Norris 26 Oct.
John Lawese 1 Nov.
Avis Odbur 11 Nov.
Christopher Baker 17 Nov.
Jane Odbur 22 Nov.
Elizabeth Jefferis 22 Nov.
Thomas Randol 15 Dec.

Mary Penny 29 Dec.
Catherine Miles 11 Jan.
Margaret Angod 27 Jan.
Alexander Randol 11 April

1682.

Hester Russel 19 May
Elizabeth Sims 20 May
Ann King 17 June
Andrew Prestly 18 June
Richard Baed 19 July
Edward Penny 8 Sep.
Sir John Saintloe 23 Oct.
Elizabeth Holly 15 Nov.
Alice Penny 2 Dec.
Henry Quinten 20 Feb.
. . . e Odbur 24 Feb.

1683.

John Randol 5 May
Jone White 29 May
Mary Huntly 27 July
Rachel Barter 11 Aug.
Ann Young 11 Aug.
Mary Marsh 4 Sep.
Hen. White 20 Oct.
Joh. Merchant 25 Oct.
John Bundy 19 Nov.
Tho. Evans 80 Dec.
Will. Penny 2 Jan.
Ann Witt 6 Jan.
Margaret Deane 12 Jan.
Joh. Witt 30 Jan.
George Lawes 31 Jan.

1684.

Margaret Penny 22 April
John Odbur 9 April
Jane Chawlk 10 May
Roger Simmons 27 Nov.
Richard Blatchford 2 Dec.
John Penny 7 Jan.
Ann Merchant 6 Jan.
Eliza. Bidlecom 21 Jan.
Sarah Hibbard 10 March

1685.

John White 16 April
Henry Mullins 25 April
Alice Penny 20 June
Joh. Lodge 4 June
Alice Penny 4 June
Mary Golding 28 July
Elizab. Lawes 23 July
Jane May 2 Aug.
Deborah Archer 15 Sep.
Ann Hartford 17 Sep.

John Penn 19 Oct.
. . . . Priest 21 Oct.
Tho. Holly 21 Nov.
Alexander ffoliat 11 Dec.
Sarah ffoxanger 26 Dec.
Mary Lawes 2 Jan.
John Skinner 7 Jan.
Elizabeth Lilly 11 Feb.

1686.

Joice Orchard 29 March
David Whitmarsh 22 April
Susanna Sloper 9 June
Sibella Gwire 27 Oct.
Elizabeth Roffe 21 Jan.
Alce ffolliat 14 Feb.
Sam. Lyle 19 March

1687.

Ann Read 4 May
Ann Randol 20 June
Joh. Stocky 21 July
Eliz. Randol 15 Nov.
Susan Gilbert 15 Nov.
Will. Brian 19 Nov.
Laurence Harvy (Fisher) 4 Jan
ffrances Bidlecom 3 Feb.
Mary Lodge 4 Feb.

1688.

Henry Norris 4 March
Jane Whitmarsh 10 May
Mary Hailock 4 June
David Rolfe 26 Sep.
Elizabeth Dew 23 Oct.
John Golden 4 Nov.
Will. Simonds 5 Dec.
Hen. Penny 7 Dec.

1689.

Joan Thorne 18 May
John Rish 26 June
John Street 18 Aug.
Henry & Moses Bedelcome 13 Oct.
Mary Stockey 17 Nov.
Jane Witt 14 Nov.

1690.

Thomas Thorne 13 May
John Semes 30 June
Richard Mullens 10 Sep.
John Rofe 10 Sep.
Thomas Penny 13 Oct.
Rose Dove 11 Nov.
Ann Stocky 10 Nov.
Marke Street 10 Jan.
Mary King 19 Jan.
William Marchant 23 Jan.

John Good 29 Jan.
Jane Smith 5 Feb.

1691.

John Sloper, Vicar 18 Oct.
Siceley Sparkes 30 Nov.
Mary Young 12 Jan.
Michall Lawes 25 Jan.

1692.

Dionissa Brine 6 April
Mrs Hatchman 30 July
Elizabeth Hassell, widow 9 Nov.
Widow Mary Saunders of Burr Chalk 6 Jan.
George Randull 28 Jan.
Isaac Miles 19 Feb.
Susanna Whitmarsh 8 March
Henry Good 20 March

1693.

Collis Penny 28 March
Ann Bennett 15 May
Elizabeth Smith 18 June
Elizabeth Bryne 15 July
John Penny 22 July
. . . . bert Wagg 17 Aug.
. . . . Odbar of the parish of Alvedeston 8 Sep.
Samuell Penny 22 Oct.
Jane Penn 18 Nov.
Ann Francis 20 Nov.
Dorothy Good 14 Dec.
Edward Allen 24 Dec.
Alice Penny 26 Dec.
Christian Archer 8 Feb.
Mr Edmond Saint Loe —Feb.
Richard Orchard 21 March

1694.

Joan Penny 19 April
Mary Dean 13 May
John Notte 16 June
John White 10 July
Ann Miles 20 Sep.
Hester Young 4 Dec.
William Penny 16 Jan.
Margaret Penny 24 Jan.
John Lodge 28 Jan.
Mary Witt 29 Jan.
John Brookman 1 Feb.
Mary White 2 Feb.
Benjamin Young 27 Feb.
Ann Read 17 March

1695.

Jane Savage 20 May
Thomas Penny 2 June

Mary Dewey 1 July
Arthur Brookman 21 July
Sarah Wagg 9 Sep.
Mᵣˢ Mary Kent 20 Nov.
Edith Lodge 7 Dec.
Mʳ Richard Sparkes 21 Dec.
Jane Street 21 Jan.
Mary Batt 12 Feb.
Philip Witt 22 March

1696.

Margaret King 1 April
Thomas Russel 2 June
Elias Ingram 6 Nov.
Eliz. Quintain 25 Nov.
John Evans 11 Dec.
William King 24 Jan.
Alice Akland 1 March
Thomas Fish 11 March

1697.

Henry Johnson 20 April
William Smith 10 May
Jone Penny 26 May
William Penny 7 June
George Akland 13 June
John Barter 8 July
Elizabeth Best 21 Nov.
Robert King 12 Dec.
William Lawes 27 Dec.
Ann Briggs 16 March

1698.

Charls Newman 25 June
Edith Nott 13 Nov.
Elizabeth Fisher 23 Nov.
Ruth Lodge 5 Jan.
Elizabeth Odbar 29 Jan.
Mʳ Ralph Good 13 Feb.
Ann Wagg 20 Feb.
Edith Newman 15 March
Jane Smith 24 March*

1699.

George Randol 3 April
Mary Richards 20 April
John Harvy 22 April
John ffarrant 29 April
John Brine 6 Aug.
Jane Stickland 2 Oct.
Abraham White 19 Oct.
William Ingram 3 Feb.
Sybilla Osmond *alias* Briggs 27 Feb.
Rachel Lodge 18 March

* Here the record of " Oaths " as to Burial in
" Woollen " ceases.

1700.

Mary Reed 25 March
Thomas Fox 4 April
Edwardus Hasell 6 Aug.
Editha Norris 6 Aug.
Francisca Gilbert 18 Aug.
Maria Silverthorn 28 Aug.
Philippa Roffe 2 Oct.
Rachel Reed 5 Oct.
Dennis Skinner 11 Oct.
Johannes Randol 21 Nov.
Georgius Antram 13 Dec.
Sarah Dean 25 Jan.
Cornelius Short 26 Feb.

1701.

Johannes Best 9 April
Johannes Folliat (seipsum strangulavit)
    9 April
Thomas Fox 19 April
Anna King 29 May
Thomas Gilbert 31 May
Timotheus Lodge 12 June
Henricus Miles 31 July
Maria Shergold w. Benjamin of the parish
    of Bishopston 20 Aug
Bartholomæus Dew 9 Oct.
Susanna Good 15 Jan.
Gulielmus King 21 Feb.
Maria Randol 24 Feb.
Roger Evans 9 March
Ann Lodge 13 March
Andrew Dean 14 March

1702.

Jone Fox 28 March
Christopher Smith 17 April
Elizabeth Hibberd 25 April
Jane Wilkins 11 May
Maria Lilly 17 June
Elizabetha Lilly 16 July
Gulielmus Segar 21 Oct.
Jane Penny 12 Nov.
Wid. Golding 13 Dec.
Maria Francis 21 Jan.
Thomas Francis (her son) same day &
    grave
Johannes Stent 17 Feb.
Henricus Good 20 Feb.
Antonius Randol 2 March
Georgius Lawes 5 March

1703.

Robertus Moulins — May
Elizabetha Fox 4 June
Elias Burton 29 June
Susanna Stockey — July

Maria Lodge 18 July
Editha Norris 21 July
Thomas Segar 23 July
Lucy Austen 27 Aug.
Gulielmus Penny 6 Sep.
Robertus Witt 10 Jan.
Katherina Witt 18 March

1704.

Laurentius Brookman 30 April
Alicia Randall, vid. 28 May
Gulielmus Gravell 11 June
Gulielmus Angood 21 July
Robertus Haylock 8 Oct.
Maria White 16 Feb.
Catherina Lawes 2 March

1705.

Richardus Spencer 1 April
Maria Ingram 1 April
Elizabetha King Lanham 29 April
Jane Mullens 9 Sep.
Henry Stickler 2 Oct.
Elizabeth Spencer 21 Oct.
William Edmonds 4 Nov.
Jane Penny 9 Nov.
John White 27 Nov.
Susanna Ingram 7 Jan.
Timothy Wag 13 Jan.
Thomas Lodge 15 Feb.

1706.

John Streete 30 March
Elizabeth Foliat 31 March
Sarah Bryne 4 April
William Fish 28 April
Mary Savage 19 May
William Odbar 8 July
Jasper Hibbert 24 Aug.
Elizabeth Goulden 10 Sep.
Anne Street 18 Sep.
Henry Watkins 20 Sep.
Henry White 25 Sep.
Edward Osment — Sep.
Abraham White — Oct.
Artillis White — Nov.
Richard Wag — Jan.
Jane Antrum — March
Mary Dun 3 March
Timothy Lodge 9 March

1707.

Mary Erwood 29 June
Jane Day 17 July
William Harford 10 Aug.
Edward Edmonds 28 Aug.
David Smith 29 Aug.

Katherine Gilbert 12 Nov.
Sarah Littlefield 25 Nov.
John Vincent 29 Dec.
Mary Lawes 28 Dec.
Thomas Francis 11 Jan.

1708.

Anne Browne 19 June
Sarah Norris 19 June
Mary Lodge 20 June
Nicholas Knot 23 June
Henry Norris 27 June
Rose Lodge 14 July
Elizabeth Odbar 25 Aug.
Thomas Gilbert 17 Sep.
Elizabeth Penny 21 Dec.
Thomas Stockey 22 Dec.
William Richards 9 Jan.
Jane Cookman 20 Jan.

1709.

Margaret King 29 March
Martha Francis 29 March
John Harford 23 May
Jane Randol 2 July
Mrs Mary Good 4 Sep.
Abraham White 2 Nov.
Thomas Gilbert 16 Jan.
William Marchant — March

1710.

Anne Lodge 9 April
Martha Gilbert 11 June
Mary Oxford 18 July
Martin Marten 16 Aug.
Elizabeth Braman 27 Aug.
William Lodge 15 Sep.
Thomas Richards 26 Sep.
Edward Penny 29 Sep.
Anne White 25 Nov.
Rebecca Fox 7 March

1711.

Hannah Harvy 31 March
Ann w. Edward Bryne 5 May
Edward Gould s. Willm. Gould 10 May
Thomas Street 3 June
Jane Penny d. Tho. Penny 3 June
Wm Gould s. William Gould 2 July
Ann Street d. Thos. & Ann 22 July
Abraham White 31 July
Edward Chalk 16 Aug.
Michal Randol w. John Randol 17 Aug.
Walter Whitmarsh of Stoke 22 Aug.
Jno. Powel 15 Oct.
Edward Hervey 20 Oct.
John Gilbert 2 Nov.

Elizabeth d. John Lawes 11 Nov.
Ann Street, widow, 14 Nov.
Philip Bennet 26 Nov.
Margaret w. Willm. Gould 10 Dec.
John Francis 31 Jan.

1712.

Robert Young s. Thos. 4 May
Jane Evans, widow, 1 June
Jane d. Edwd. & Mary Witt 21 June
Tho. s. Thomas Peny 19 Nov.
Robert Briant — Feb.

1713.

Samuel King — April
Mary d. Laurence Harvy — May
Thomas Brown — June
John Bishop s. Ann Short — July
Jane w. Wᵐ Dean — Sep.
——— w. Edʷᵈ Penny ———
. . . . n Laws — Oct.
. . . . ry Cook — Oct.
Dennis w. Alexander King — Oct.
Ann Allen — Nov.
Eleanor Quintin w. Henry — Nov.
Dennis Powell, widow, — Feb.
Thomas Fish — Feb.
Eleanor Richards, widow, 12 March
Jane Jennings w. Jacob Jennings 18 Mar

1714.

Walter Combes of Wilton 4 April
Mary w. Edʷᵈ Penny 23 June
John Lilly 31 July
Mary Frances, widow, 19 Sep.
Henry Biddlecomb — Oct.
Martha w. John Lodge 15 Nov.
Sarah w. Samuel Penny — Nov.
Mary w. John Penny 30 Jan.
John Penny 8 Feb.
Avice Batt, widow, 14 Feb.

1715.

George s. George Best 4 April
Jane White of Sarum 28 April
Elizabeth d. Tho. Young 7 May
Ann w. Peregrine Dove 15 May
John Frampton 29 May
Robert s. Thomas Young 7 June
Joyce w. Wᵐ Whitmarsh 15 Aug.
Mary d. Henry Randol 5 Oct.
Thomas Randol 20 Jan.
Mary Segar, widow, 24 Feb.
William s. William Fox 14 March

1716.

Mary Williams d. Henry 2 April
Joseph Savage 14 April

William Smith 6 May
Susan Fish, widow, 15 May
Susanna w. Willm. Andrews — May
William Andrews — June
Joan Biddlecomb, widow, — July
William s. Wᵐ Langtry 21 Sep.
Jane w. Tho. Johnson 3 Nov.
Thomas s. Samuel White 12 Nov.
Ann d. Richard Roberts 26 Nov.
Edward Brine — Dec.
Patience d. Phebe Rains 6 Jan.
William Harford 24 Feb.
Henry Penny 21 Feb.

———

*Martha d. Willᵐ Speering — Nov.
*Ambrose Richards 11 Dec.
*John Ingram 25 Dec.
*Eliz. King, widow, 23 March

1720.

Lucy d. Edward Perry 23 May
Ann Savage 24 May
Elizabeth w. Tho. Read 1 July
Elizabeth d. Thomas Penny 4 Dec.
Thomas Reed 30 Dec.
William s. Thomas Moody 18 Feb.

1721.

Jane d. William Everley 28 March
Margaret d. Jacob Jennings 6 April
Dennis w. John Russell 17 April
Margaret w. Jacob Jennings 25 April
Joseph s. Tho. Vincent 8 June
Edward Penny 14 Nov.
John s. William Speering 23 Nov.
Ann d. Samuel Penny 26 Nov.
Bridget Gould, widow, 12 March
Eleanor Short, widow, 12 March

1722.

John Russell 2 May
John White 10 May
John s. Thomas Laws 29 May
George s. George Reed 26 July
Robert s. Thomas Moody 11 Aug.
Jeremiah Penny 16 Oct.
Sarah d. Richard Lush 16 Nov.
Dorothy w. Richard Lush 17 Nov.
Elizabeth Bound w. William 8 Dec.
Richard Lush 11 Dec.
Mary d. William Bound 23 Dec.
Mary w. Thomas Laws 2 Jan.
Joyce w. Robert Witt 14 Jan.

* These four entries probably belong to 1719, as
a page is evidently missing from the Register.

Sarah w. Thomas Laws 21 Jan.
Artillis White, widow, 7 Feb.
Ann Foliot, widow, 27 Feb.
William Everley 4 March
Jacob s. Jacob Jennings 18 March

1723.

John Barnes s. John 9 April
Robert Witt 14 April
Catherine Hutchins 5 May
William Speering 22 May
Judith Savage, widow, — May
Elisabeth d. Thomas Smith 8 Aug.
Timothy Lodge 15 Aug.
Elisabeth w. John Lewin 22 Aug.
Christobell Harford, widow, 28 Sep.
Jane Spencer 14 Oct.
Jane d. David Skinner 23 Oct.
John s. Edward Harvey 11 Nov.
Mary Ingram 12 Nov.
John s. of John Ford of Allhallows 26 Nov.
Jacob s. Jacob Jennings 2 Jan.
Jacob Jennings 7 Dec.
Ann d. Jacob Jennings 11 Dec.
Elizabeth w. Henry Peny 3 Jan.
William Biggs 11 Feb.

1724.

George s. Henry Randol 2 June
Lucy d. Alexander King 15 June
Elisabeth d. John Day 15 July
Margaret d. Randol Lodge 21 July
Thomas Young 30 Aug.
Dennis Ingram 19 Sep.
Jane Loader — Oct.
James s. Edward Savage 13 Oct.
Elizabeth Randol, widow, 6 Nov.
Mary Witt, widow, 13 Nov.
William Lilly 14 Nov.
Sarah Foliat 19 Nov.
Avis Bryant, widow, 27 Jan.
Hannah d. John Stockey 2 March
Eliz^th w. Laurence Brookman 15 March

1725.

William s. Dinah Lilly, widow, 2 April
James Prince 25 May
Charles s. William & Elisabeth Smith 15 June
Elisabeth d. Laurence & Jane Harvey — Sep.
Hannah w. Edward Savage 27 Sep.
Mary d. James Strickland 16 Nov.
Jane Norris 17 Nov.
Mary d. Henry Cook 20 Nov.
Jane d. Ann Savidge 26 Nov.

Jane w. Laurence Harvey 12 Dec.
Eliz. Dean 28 Dec.

1725-6.

Thomas Bates 25 Jan.
Robert s. Thomas Moody — Jan.
Sarah Biggs 12 Feb.
Richard Barter 18 Feb.

1726.

Alexander King 4 April
Randolph Lodge 5 May
Edith Lodge 5 May
Ann d. Randolph Lodge 11 May
Sarah & Susannah dd. Eliz. Speering 11 May
Thomas Laws 14 May
John Penn buried without the Church Service 14 May
Charles s. Thomas Batt 15 June
Henry s. Henry Cook 17 June
William s. Henry Cook 24 June
Jane d. George Laws 10 Oct.
William Chalk 22 Nov.
Elizabeth Penny 29 Jan.
Thomas Vincent 13 Feb.
Henry Randall 23 Feb.

1727.

Hannah Harvey 26 April
Catharine Biggs 16 May
Anne Ingram 6 June
Edward Harvey 21 June
William Young 24 Aug.
Elisabeth Read 30 Oct.
Henry Quintain 9 Nov.
Edward Penny 10 Nov.
Charles Good (of ye parish of Devyses) 11 Nov.
Thomas s. Jane Cookman 19 Dec.
Jane w. Richard King 25 Dec.
Thomas Lodge 3 Jan.
Mary King 17 Dec.
James s. Ralph & Ruth Streight 20 Feb.
Thomas Johnson 11 March

1728.

Alice Barter 11 April
Thomas Penny 13 April
Anne Roaf 14 April
William Fox 16 April
William Whitmarsh 8 May
Elisabeth Woodward w. — Woodward of Sarum — July
Sarah d. Richard & Mary Stent ———
John Bryne ———
Anne Bunter w. Thomas 29 Nov.

James s. Thomas & Mary King 15 Dec.
Sarah Gould w. Robt Gould 21 Jan. 172⅚
Rachel Lodge 3 Feb.
Thomas Penny 2 March
Thomas s. George & Sarah Read 10 March

1729.

Joane Angood 7 April
Mary Lodge 27 April
Edith d. Willm. & Edith Angood 28 April
Anne d. Henry & Jane King 5 May
Robert s. Philippa Angood 6 May
Sarah d. David & Mary Charel 17 May
William s. William & Mary King 25 May
Thomas King 26 June
Elisabeth w. Will'm Smith 22 July
Elias Ingram 18 Aug.
Sarah d. Tho. & Jane Laws 16 Oct.
Thomas Wag 27 Oct.
Richard Sparks 29 Nov.
Jane w. David Skinner 15 Dec.
Mary d. David Skinner 22 Dec.
Sarah Batts 25 Dec.
William Dean 20 Jan.
Denyse Ingram 4 Feb.
Thomas s. George & Sarah Read 6 Feb.
John Card 15 Feb.
George Antrim 22 Feb.
William Sager 19 March
Jane w. George Turner Senr 23 March

1730.

Mary Viny 29 March
Jane King 9 April
Mary Antrim 29 April
Henry King 19 May
John Laws 19 June
Henry s. Henry & Elis. Randol 30 July
Mary d. Thomas & Elisabeth Penn 19 Aug.
John s. John Lodge 25 Sep.
Elisabeth Quintin 27 Oct.
Richard s. Rich^d & Betty Foliat 4 Dec.
Jane Lowther 25 Dec.
Jane d. Thomas & Jane Penny 5 Jan.
Mary w. Gilbert Dod 26 Feb.
Jane Andrews 3 March
Anne d. John & Mary Powel 15 March

1731.

Dorothy Hasel — March
Anne w. Thomas Moody — April
Joyce Penn 23 April
Elisabeth w. Mr Tho. Penn 9 May
Laurence Harvey 4 June
Jane w. John Reynes 12 June
Elisabeth Lilly 12 June
Mr John Coombs 15 June

Deborah White 16 June
Hannah Savage 25 June
Sarah d. Henry Randol 28 June
Jane w. Anthony Penny 10 July
William Best 13 July
George Read 10 Aug.
George s. William & Mary Laws 27 Aug.
Mary w. William Laws 30 Aug.
Mary d. Robert & Mary Fox 3 Sep.
Alexander King 6 Sep.
Catharine w. James Strickland 11 Oct.
James s. James & Joyce Strickland 12 Feb.
A male Infant of Henry Penny Junr

1732.

Edward Witt 31 March
Mary d. John & Mary Laws 4 April
Jane w. Alexander Penny 21 April
Jane Penny 7 April
Lucy Yateman 20 May
Patience w. John Merchant 10 Aug.
Sarah Chalk 7 Sep.
Anne Edmunds 8 Oct.
Henry Penny 10 Oct.
Edward s. Henry & Martha Cook 2 Dec.
William Cookman 30 Dec.
Barbara King 19 Jan.

1733.

Robert Laws 1 April
George Laws 10 April
Hannah Cookman 25 April
Hannah w. Henry Penny 26 April
Joan w. Laurence Brookman 8 May
Mary d. Miles & Elisabeth Northover 12 May
Stephen Hort 23 May
William s. Robert & Mary Fox 4 June
Mary d. William & Jane Langtry 2 July
Mary w. David Gerard 8 Aug.
Richard King 19 Sep.
John Cookman 28 Sep.
Anne w. George Golden 3 Oct.
Mary Penn 18 Nov.
Elisabeth d. Henry Penny 14 Feb.

1734.

Jane bast. d. Jane Penny ——
Elisabeth d. John & Elisabeth Gibbs ——
Mary w. Philip Kirley ——
Mary Dove 29 Sep.
Jane & Roger s. & d. Tho. & Esther Jolly 9 Oct.
Martha w. Nicolas Savage 26 Oct.
Jane White 29 Oct.
Lucy Angood 1 Nov.

Sarah d. Thomas & Anne Hesket 5 Nov.
Lucy d. Philip Kirley 24 Feb.
William Bennet 4 March

1735.

John White 27 March
Mary d. John Merchant 28 March
Henry s. Henry & Mary Williams 1 May
Susan Vincent 5 May
John Penny 27 May
Mrs Mary w. George Penruddock Esq. 20 June
William s. William Viny 28 June
John s. John & Mary Barnet 29 July
Anne Spencer from Burr Chalk 28 Aug.
George Antrim from Burr Chalk 8 Oct.
Sarah d. William & Sarah Haywood 3 Dec.
John Powel 3 Dec.
Jane d. Henry & Jane Stainer 23 Dec.
Michal Scaplin 15 Jan.
Stephen s. David & Anne Smith 21 Jan.
Robert Gold 10 Feb.

1736.

Sarah d. William & Betty Scammel 27 April
Miles s. Miles & Elisabeth Northover 27 April
Joyse Witt 7 Aug.
Mr Charles Good 29 Sep.
Jane w. Thomas Laws 29 Sep.
Martha w. William Hartford 27 Dec.
Anne Guyer 28 Dec.
Laurence Brookman 9 Jan.
Anne Read 16 March

1737.

Philip s. John & Milliere Angood 29 Mar.
William King from the Hut 7 April
George Golden 15 April
Sarah Ford 22 April
Samuel White 10 May
John s. Jasper Whitmarsh 13 July
Anne w. Thomas Street 22 July
William Crume killed by a waggon 28 July
Sarah Laws 19 Aug.
Miles s. Miles & Elisabeth Northover 26 Aug.
Henry Williams 8 Sep.
Elisabeth w. William Scammel 15 Sep.
Philippa w. William Frecker 12 Oct.
Christiane w. Henry Kirley 12 Nov.
Mary d. Thomas Street 17 Nov.
Mrs Jane Combs 22 Nov.
William s. Robert & Mary Fox 25 Nov.
Mary Adlam 7 Dec.
Jane w. George Laws — Dec.

. . . . h d. Willm. & Sarah Hayward — Dec.
William s. Henry & Jane Stayner 1 March
Elisabeth d. Thomas & Mary Smith 8 March
Mr Thomas Penn 15 March

1738.

Jane d. Aaron & Jane Thompson 1 April
David Skinner 5 April
Thomas Ingram 18 May
Henry Cook 4 Sep.
Elisabeth w. Robert Witt 7 Oct.
Thomas s. John & Jane Witt 14 Nov.
Jane w. John Barns 16 Nov.
John Lodge 5 Dec.
Elisabeth Francis 12 Feb.
Joan w. William Chalk 21 March

1739.

Elisabeth Tolley 10 April
Mary d. George Laws 27 April
Martha King 28 April
Robert s. John Williams 30 April
Henry Randol 25 May
Anne Savage 23 July
Charles s. William Hartford 7 Sep.
Willm. s. John & Hannah Laws 30 Sep.
George s. John & Mary Abbot 4 Dec.
Charles Savage 9 Jan.
John Northover 21 Jan.
Christopher Toogood 8 March
Mrs Elisabeth w. Mr Thomas Moody 18 March

1740.

Jane Richards 24 April
Elisabeth d. Walter & Martha Whitmarsh 27 April
Hugh Mills 19 May
Anne White 7 June
Mr Thomas Dunfort 9 June
Robert s. John & Anne Williams 30 June
Mary d. James & Anne Smith 22 July
Elisabeth Speering 23 July
Anne w. Nicolas White 26 July
Roger Barns Senr 11 Oct.
Jane w. Thomas Ingram 31 Oct.
Anne White from Handly 13 Nov.
Jane Johnson 27 Nov.
Philip Kirley 29 Nov.
Henry Penny 23 Feb.
William Bryan 5 March
Jane Card 11 March

1741.

Jane Randol 24 June

John Angood 16 July
William s. William & Anne Stevens 29
    July
Martha Wagg 2 Aug.
Mary Northover 25 Aug.
Jane Richards 27 Aug.
Jane King — Aug.
Jane w. Thomas Penny — Oct.
John Randol 29 Oct.
George Turner 17 Dec.
Jane Seager 17 Dec.
Joseph s. Edward Savage 11 March

1742.

Jane d. Walter & Martha Whitmarsh 3
    May
Stephen s. Robert & Mary Fox 5 May
William s. William & Mary King 7 June
Robert s. John & Mary Penny 1 Aug.
Elisabeth Snooks 24 Aug.
Rose d. John & Elisabeth Young 21 Sep.
John Seager 24 Oct.
David Smith 29 Oct.
William Fox 1 Jan.
Anne w. David Smith 27 Jan.
John s. John & Mary Penny 31 Jan.
Henry s. Willm & Sarah Butcher 5 Feb.
William s. Benjamin & Jane Johnson 6
    Feb.
Sarah d. David & Anne Smith 10 Feb.
Joseph s. Thomas & Mary Smith 15 Feb.
John Angood 27 Feb.
Anne d. Jasper & Elisabeth Whitmarsh
    18 March

1743.

William Chalk 30 March
Thomas Ford 12 May
George s. Ellis & Elisabeth Ingram 18 May
Sarah d. Caleb & Tabitha Cavil 12 June
Jane d. David Smith 16 June
Mary d. John & Jane Witt 26 June
Thomas Randol 4 July
George Randol 11 Aug.
Elisabeth Randol 20 Sep.
Repentance Dun 15 Oct.
Elisabeth w. Edward Frampton 16 Oct.
John Barnes 19 Jan.
John s. Mr Thomas Moody 26 Jan.
Henry bast. s. Martha Savage 9 Feb.
John s. John & Mary Dibben 4 March

1744.

Robert & Thomas ss. William & Elisabeth
    Northover 8 April
Mary w. John Perry 1 May
Milliere Angood 18 May

William s. William & Martha Penny 18
    May
Sarah w. William Hayward 13 June
Robert Best of Ebbsbourn 21 June
Joseph s. Bravall & Mary West 14 July
Alexander Penny 15 July
Sarah Chalk 28 Aug.
Thomas Penny 9 Sep.
Anne Street 28 Sep.
Sarah d. Thomas & Mary Moody 16 Nov.
Alice Grey 20 Nov.
Samuel Penny 28 Jan.
Elisabeth Laws — Feb.
John Rains 9 March

1745.

Dinah Lilly 31 March
William King 23 April
James s. John & Elisabeth Young 1 June
Mary Fox 12 June
Elisabeth w. Miles Northover 28 June
Charles s. Charles & Mary Hiscock 20 Aug.
William s. John & Mary Dibbens 27 Aug.
Henry Penny 8 Sep.
Henry Norris 9 Oct.
Edward Fish 27 Nov.
James Strickland 12 Jan.
Henry Stockey 22 Jan.
Thomas Street 12 March

1746.

Joseph Gold 29 March
Anne d. John Gibbs 6 April
Susanna Savage 29 April
Mr Henry Good of Hatch 13 June
Hannah d. Edward Savage 22 June
Thomas Binney a stranger who died on
    the road 27 July
William Smith 21 Aug.
Jane w. David Gerard 6 Oct.
Mary Witt 18 Oct.
Charles Hartford 19 Oct.
Susanna d. Thomas & Rebecca Read 29
    Oct.
Jane King 9 March
Mary w. Thomas Moody 14 March

1747.

Nicolas Savage 27 March
Sarah d. John & Anne Williams 22 May
Anne w. William Stephens 25 May
Aimy d. George Penruddock Esq. 30 May
Elisabeth w. George Turner Junr 9 June
William Biggs 30 June
Mary w. John Hazel of Fifield 6 July
Joan Fox 28 July
Anne Fish 21 Aug.

Anne d. William & Sarah King 22 Aug.
Elisabeth Thick 18 Oct.
Mary d. Luke & Esther Francis 21 Oct.
Sarah Biggs 24 Oct.
Ruth White from Alvedeston 3 Nov.
Martha Cook 3 Nov.
M**rs** Jane Dunford 1 Feb.
John Roberts 23 March

1748.

Elisabeth w. Robert Merchant 20 May
George Penruddock Esq. 24 May
Ruth d. John & Honour Pin 6 June
Betty d. George Turner 13 June
Thomas Hort 2 July
Sarah d. John & Mary Dibbens — July
William s. Stephen & Mary Smith — Aug.
Betty d. John & Betty Young ———
Nathanael s. William & Mary Crine ———
Katharine d. of Nicolas & Hannah White
    15 Oct.
Sarah d. William & Jane Langtry 1 Nov.
Mary Laws 21 Nov.
John s. John & Jane Grey 29 Nov.
M**r** Ralph Good 28 Feb.
Joseph s. John & Honour Pin 1 March

1749.

David Penny 30 March
Thomas Read 6 April
Robert Hort 20 June
Elisabeth w. John Young 7 Aug.
Roger Beling 18 Sep.
Charles Hiscock 18 Oct.
Grace w. Thomas Northover 23 Nov.
Joan Savage 16 Jan.
Esther w. Thomas Jolliffe 27 Jan.
Elisabeth widow of William Smith 7 Feb.
Anne w. William Johnson 12 Feb.
William Randol 13 Feb.
Jane w. John Penny 16 Feb.
George Turner 24 March

1750.

Mary d. John & Elisabeth Emme 16 April
Henry s. John & Ann Everet 23 April
John s. Henry & Jane Stainer 23 May
Elisabeth Fox 18 June
Henry Angood 20 June
Mary Laws 30 Aug.
Josiah s. Thomas & Mary Gold 30 Sep.
Abigail w. George Bradley 12 Oct.
Dinah Elderton from Bishopston 29 Oct.
Elisabeth Garret 9 Jan.
Martha & Mary dd. John & Jane Smith
    27 Jan.
Thomas Barnes 12 Feb.

1751.

Elisabeth w. Jasper Whitmarsh 2 April
Charles s. William & Martha Penny 23
    April
Mary wife George Sansom 27 May
John s. John & Jane Rolf 2 July
Rev**d** Aaron Thompson, Vicar 1 Aug.
Sarah Randol, widdow 3 Nov.
John Gibs 12 Nov.
James Perry 17 Nov.

1752.

Joan Mills 19 Jan.
Anne d. Robert & Jane Penny 26 Jan.
Mary w. Richard Stent 29 Jan.
Sarah d. Willm. & Sarah King, the Hut,
    26 April
John s. Willm. & Mary Tudgey 16 Sep.
Ann Dean, widow 18 Sep.

1753. N.S.

Ann King 3 Jan.
John Angood 1 May
Mary d. Edward & Ann Hardyman June
James s. John & Bridget Perry 28 June
Mary Ingram 8 July
Robert Merchant 11 Aug.
Edith Angood 2 Oct.
William Harris 31 Oct.

1754.

John s. Samuel & Diana King 12 Feb.
John Roaf 24 March
James s. William & Mary Tudgey 22
    April
Mary w. George Lawes 11 May
Mary Ingram 9 June
Ann w. Edward Hardyman 21 Sep.
John s. Edward & Ann Hardyman 28 Sep.
David Skinner (from Wiley) 13 Oct.
Martha Cook 28 Oct.
Elizabeth w. Thomas Batt 5 Nov.
Thomas s. Thomas & Mary Batchelor 26
    Dec.
Thomas Turner 31 Dec.

1755.

Mary Hiscock 1 Jan.
Jane d. Anthony Penny 3 Jan.
Rebecca Laws 4 Jan.
Mary Smith base-born d. Mary King 15
    Jan.
Mary w. John Powel 21 Jan.
Betty d. John & Ann Everet 29 Jan.
Harry s. William & Elizabeth King 8
    April

Mary King 4 June
Rose base-born d. Joyce Beling 8 June
Anne w. John Day 17 Oct.
William s. Thomas & Elizabeth Cook 29
    Oct.
Henry King, sen[r] from the Hut 30 Oct.
Ruth Antrim, widow, 11 Nov.
Mary King, widow, 20 Nov.
Harry s. Robert & Jane Penny 21 Dec.
Samuel King 28 Dec.

1756.

Mary Roaf, widow, 1 Jan.
John Roaf 10 Jan.
Jane Street, widow, 19 Feb.
Mary w. Thomas Gould 10 March
Elizabeth Gould 9 April
M[rs] Edith Good, widow, 14 May
Elizabeth d. Thomas & Martha Hayden
    27 May
Mary Harford 20 June
Sarah d. Charles & Mary Smith 13 July
George s. Henry & Elizabeth Jay 25 July
Mary w. John Hazel, from Fifield, 2 Aug.
Christobel Harford 22 Dec.

1757.

Ann w. John Grey 8 Jan.
Jeremiah s. Thomas & Alice Teague 10
    Jan.
Jane d. Christopher & Eleanor Stone 21
    Jan.
Martha w. Walter Whitmarsh 24 Jan.
George Wood 11 Feb.
William s. John & Mary Dibben 13 April
William s. William & Mary James 24
    April
Edith Best, widow, 1 May
Ann d. John & Ann Williams 12 May
Joyce w. Walter Beling 16 July
William Harford 7 Sep.
Urella d. Henry & Hannah White 30 Sep.
Sarah d. John & Bridget Perry 28 Oct.
Thomas s. Henry & Elizabeth Jay 30 Oct.
Betty d. John & Jane Grey 5 Nov.
M[r] Timothy Lodge 30 Nov.

1758.

Anthony Penny 3 Jan.
Jasper Whitmarsh 12 Jan.
Alexander s. William & Mary Stephens
    14 Jan.
Jane w. Henry Stainer 7 April
Ann w. Thomas Major 18 April
Mary w. James Deane 16 June
Betty d. John & Mary Stephens 29 June
William Johnson 2 July

Hannah w. Henry White 22 Aug.
Robina Turner, widow, 28 Aug.
Richard Carey 16 Oct.
John Stocky 13 Nov.
Mary d. John & Mary Lawes 30 Dec.

1759.

Jane w. Benjamin Johnson 1 Jan.
Elizabeth d. William & Elizabeth Shepherd
    16 Jan.
Walter Whitmarsh 11 Feb.
Mary Harford, widow, 4 April
Elizabeth d. Thomas & Judith Trowbridge
    8 Aug.
John s. James Deane 14 Aug.
Richard s. Paul & Hannah Scammel 4
    Dec.
Thomas Major 9 Dec.
Leah d. Charles & Hannah Smith 21 Dec.

1760.

James s. Henry & Mary Strickland 16 Jan.
Henry Penn 25 Feb.
George Golding 26 April
Ann Russell 21 May
John Gerard 10 June
Nanny Stephens 12 June
Thomas Lawes 18 June
Alice Perry 13 July
Elizabeth d. Richard & Sarah Toomer 3
    Aug.
Thomas s. Thomas & Mary Batchelor 5
    Sep.
Thomas Gould 28 Sep.
Jane d. John & Jane Grey Nov.
Henry s. Richard & Jane Read 9 Dec.

1761.

Thomas Batchelor 2 Jan.
Thomas Lawes 7 Jan.
Robert Best 1 Feb.
Elizabeth w. John Cook 11 Feb.
Thomas Smith 3 March
Benjamin Best 17 March
Elizabeth w. Garret Dean 23 March
Henry s. David & Sarah Long 18 April
William Toomer 12 June
Henry s. David & Ann Gerard 6 July
William s. William & Elizabeth King 19
    July
Mary Wagg 25 July
Mary d. John & Elizabeth Emme 20 Aug.
Elizabeth d. William & Elizabeth Shepherd
    7 Sep.
Sarah d. Mary Mitchel 11 Nov.
Elizabeth w. Richard Barter 12 Dec.
Elizabeth Bradly 20 Dec.

1762.

Jeffery Moody 2 Jan.
James Northover 23 Jan.
Rebecca Gould, widow, 13 Feb.
William s. Mr William Gifford 14 March
Mary Jennings 28 March
Ann w. John Yates 2 May
Ann Catford 13 July
William s. William & Mary James 19 July
Elizabeth Cook, a child, 26 Oct.
Mary Smith of Stoke, a child, 31 Oct.
Henry White, senr 2 Nov.
Ruth Street of Stoke 7 Nov.
William Tudgy 19 Nov.
Sarah Toomer, a child, of Stoke 20 Nov.
Jane Smith of Stoke 23 Nov.
William Hayward of Stoke 23 Nov.
Sarah Hawkins of Stoke 24 Nov.
David Long 25 Nov.
Elizabeth Folliot 2 Dec.
Richard Folliot, her son, 2 Dec.
Elizabeth Penny 6 Dec.
Jane Roaf 7 Dec.
George Read of Stoke 9 Dec.
William Deane 15 Dec.
Ruth Street, junr of Stoke 15 Dec.
Sarah Wilkins of Stoke 15 Dec.
William Northover 18 Dec.
Thomas Northover 20 Dec.
Sarah Northover, his wife 20 Dec.
Mary Norris of Stoke Dec.
Jane Deane Dec.
Mrs Thomson, widow of the Revd Mr Thomson, Vicar of this Parish, from Fovant 29 Dec.
John s. John & Mary Hasel 29 Dec.

1763.

William Laws 4 Jan.
Rebecca w. Josias Gould 5 Jan.
John Day 8 Jan.
Mr Thomas Ledge 11 Jan.
George Cox 2 March
George Turner 14 March
Mary Smith 17 March
John Pin 29 March
William Shepherd, an Infant, May 2
Henry White 8 May
Diana Sophia Northover, an Infant, 30 Aug.
Thomas s. Wm & Eliz. Shepherd 10 Sep.
Elizabeth w. Wm Turner, from Chettle 19 Oct.
Richard Stent of Stoke 21 Oct.
Mr Gifford 24 Dec.
Thomas Vincent 30 Dec.

1764.

Sarah King 4 Feb.
George Bradley 14 March
Thos. Cook's child 27 March
James Combes 6 Sep.
Judith Savidge 24 Sep.
Thos. Trowbridge's child 28 Oct

1765.

Henry Stainer 6 Aug.
John Goodson 23 Sep.
John Merchant 24 Sep.
Wm James 6 Oct
Susanna Adlom 13 Feb.
William Langtry 4 April
Ann Guwyer 22 Oct.
Sarah Long 5 Nov.
Betty King 25 Oct.
Betty Northover 28 Nov.
Henry Penney 28 Nov.
Grace Penney 22 Dec.
Wm Russell 25 Dec.

1766.

Wm King 4 Jan.
Elias Ingram 20 Jan.
Betty Smith 27 Jan.
Joseph Gerrard 15 Feb.
Elizabeth Trubridge 19 Feb.
Mrs Ann Chaffy 29 March
Wm Turner 26 April
John Biggs 1 May
Luke Frances 19 May
Ralph Good 2 June
Walter Belon 11 June
Henry Savidge 16 Aug.
John Perry 4 Sep.
John Hazel 6 Oct.
Jane Miles 9 Oct.
Elizabeth Savidge 19 Oct.
Thos. Batt 26 Oct.
Wm Shepherd 29 Oct.
Jane Grey 2 Dec.

1767.

Sarah Read 1 Jan.
Sarah King 26 Jan.
Robt. Whit 6 Feb.
George Read 2 May
David Lawes 26 June
Thos. Wilkins 10 July
Anstice Lawrence 11 July
George Northover 15 July
Hannah Lodge 23 July
Richard Barter 3 Aug.
Nancy Smith 21 Aug.
John Lawes 27 Oct.

Ann Jolliffe 4 Dec.
Thos. Vincent 31 Dec.

1768.

Ann King 14 Jan.
Seymor Harris 18 Jan.
Jane Langtry 1 Feb.
Eliz. Parrot 6 March
Joseph Combes 25 March
Edward Perry 7 May
Mary Barter 29 May
Eliz. Read June
Mary Northover 14 July
Deborah Burton 3 Aug.
Elizabeth Ingram 2 Nov.

1769.

Ruth Cook 9 Jan.
Thos. Gould 10 Jan.
Jane Street 19 Feb.
James Chant 24 March
Sarah Langtry 3 April
Sarah Clerk 12 May
Ralph Street 5 July
Wᵐ Tudgey 25 July
Josiah Burton 16 Aug.
Mary Ann Penny 22 Aug.
John Burton 24 Aug.
Jane Dibbon 25 Aug.
Sarah Burton 27 Aug.
Ann Pinn 1 Sep.
Eliz. Parrot 1 Oct.
Edith Best 5 Oct.
Eliz. Vincent 16 Oct.
James Foyle 9 Dec.
Edward Woodlands 25 Dec.

1770.

Sarah Witmarsh 9 Jan.
Ann Jeffery 14 Jan.
Mary Barter 17 Jan.
Mary Hulet 25 Jan.
Sarah Cox 26 Jan.
Tabitha Cavill 12 Feb.
Elizabeth Cook 15 March
John Brookman 17 April
Edward Savidge 26 April
Ann Emm 6 June
John Street 22 Oct.
Jane Penny 27 Oct.
Elizabeth Biggs 6 Nov.
Ann Hasel 21 Nov.
John Coltstreem 29 Nov.

1771.

John Penny 9 Jan.
Thos. Ingram 6 March

Rachel Witmarsh 9 March
Jane Foyle 9 March
Mary Sampson 19 March
John Lawes 24 April
Wᵐ Stephens 27 April
John Hulet 17 June
John Compton August
John Dixon Oct.
Thos. Hayden 28 Oct.
Mary Crine 30 Oct.
Mary Pen 7 Nov.

1772.

Mary Smith 22 Jan.
John Golden 27 Jan.
Betty Ember 28 March
George Northover 6 April
James Upjohn 12 April
Dinah Witmarsh 21 June
Elizabeth Foyle 7 Nov.

1773.

Martha Marchent 3 Jan.
Jeremiah Soff 21 Jan.
Darkes King 21 Jan.
John Mills 28 Jan.
Mary Foyle 11 Feb.
James Langtry 16 March
John Burton 4 April
Mary Perry 19 May
Diana King 7 June
John Penny 17 July
Elinor Combes 16 Nov.
John Stockey 24 Nov.

1774.

Christian Moor 10 Jan.
Revᵈ Mʳ Lewelin, (Curate of this Parish)
    3 March
John Umfries 16 March
Anne Stockey 11 May
John Hazel 11 July
Mary Gifford 13 July
Thomas Emm 14 Sep.
Thomas Parrot 2 Nov.
John Gould 17 Nov.
Elizabeth Parrot 10 Dec.

1775.

Jane Lush 20 Jan.
Mary Pasons 23 April
David Jeret 29 April
Love Peram 20 July
Bety Stephins 25 July
James Peny 26 July
Anne Foil July
John Ingram July

1776.

Bety Bungy 10 Jan.
James Feltham 18 Jan.
Jane Feltham 24 Jan.
Jane Biggs 5 Feb.
Anne Feltham 5 Feb.
Jane Langtry 26 Feb.
Anne King 14 March
James Turner 22 March
Henry Good 29 March
Joice Sticklen 15 April
William Northover 11 May
Mary Dove 16 Aug.
Georg Pinn 19 Aug.
Mary Chant 22 Aug.
Mary Batchelor 12 Nov.
Licy Witte 16 Nov.
Bety Gosmey 3 Dec.
Raynold Randol 22 Dec.

1777.

John Burton 23 Jan.
Mary Frances 26 Jan.
Thomas Jolliffe 21 Feb.
Sarah Turner 17 May
Rebecca Read 14 July
John Dibon 20 July
John Knight 27 July
Anne King 2 Aug.
Richard Lush 7 Aug.
Anne Dibon 16 Aug.
Henry Jeret 4 Sep.
Anne Jeret 29 Sep.
David Jeret 6 Oct.
Elizabeth Emm 6 Nov.

1778.

Wᵐ Crine 7 Jan.
Mary Fox 17 Jan.
Jane Angood 20 Feb.
John Ingram 2 March

Anne Chant 4 March
John Biggs 6 May
Elizabeth Emm 3 Sep.
Elizabeth Gibbs 24 Sep.
John Fifield 22 Oct.
Elizabeth Fifield 13 Dec.

1779.

Mary Crine 8 Jan.
John Cook 27 Jan.
Jane Witt 13 Feb.
Dorcas Perry 4 March
Eli Emm 24 March
James Perry 2 April
Caleb Cavel 10 May
James Frances 4 July
Thos. Langtry 29 July
Jane Shepard 20 Aug.
Catherine Shepard 22 Aug.
John Penny 22 Aug.
Sarah Mussel 1 Sep.
Betty Jay 10 Sep.
Mary Jolliffe 16 Sep.
John Jaret 20 Sep.
Sarah Hulet 27 Sep.
Mary Jay 7 Oct.
Sarah Jay 12 Oct.
Mary Sansom 15 Nov.
Charles Lush 7 Dec.

1780.

Henry King 16 Jan.
James Perry 4 Feb.
John Witt 12 Feb.
Mary Whitmarsh 19 Feb.
John Francis 27 Feb.
Sarah Randol 13 May
Anne Ingram — July
Elizabeth Harford 12 July
Henry King 20 July
Rebecca Jay 7 Aug.
Mary Crouch 24 Nov.

MARRIAGES.

1725.

Thomas King & Mary Angood 7 April

172⅚.

Edward Savidge & Judith Savidge 13 Feb.

1726.

John Biggs & Catherine Gwyer both of Stoke 17 July

William King & Mary Fay 12 Oct.

1727.

John Gibbs & Elisabeth Read 29 May

William Bown & Mary Penny 19 Feb.

1728.

William Laws & Mary Russell 20 July

Walter Beling & Joyce Penn 28 Sep.

Laurence Brookman & Joan Young 6 Oct.

1729.

Laurence Thick & Elisabeth Antrim by a Licence 26 March

Richard Foliat & Betty Penny 24 April

John Longman & Frances Ansty both of Alveston 14 Oct.

1730.

Joseph Combe & Eleanor Vincent 21 Sep.

William Hewlet & Mary Richards 27 Sep.

John Wheeler of Pentridge & Mary Day of Burr Chalk 21 Oct.

Miles Northover & Elisabeth Savage 2 Nov.

John Merchant & Patience Witt 20 Dec.

1731.

William Northover & Betty Witt 5 June

Thomas Weeks & Sarah Hayter of Downton by Licence 27 Oct.

1732.

William Laws & Mary Adlam 10 April

William Viny & Honour Biddlecome 31 Aug.

Thomas Hesket & Anne Penny 1 Oct.

William Scammel & Betty Laws 14 Jan.

1733.

William Butcher & Sarah Biggs 24 May

John Penny & Jane Sanger both of East Knoyle by Licence 3 Oct.

William Hatch of Brampshare & Sarah Holliday of Newbridge, Hamp. by Licence 21 Dec.

John Yates of Fonthill & Mary Speering of this Parish 10 Feb.

1734.

David Gerard & Jane Spencer 23 April

Roger Beling of this Parish & Mary Williams of Woodgreen in the Forest 24 April

George Laws & Anne Jay 28 Sep.

John Havard of Barford & Martha Whitmarsh 11 Nov.

Gehazi Baker & Anne Stent 15 Nov.

Alexander Penny & Joan Wheeler 17 Nov.

William Slabs & Sarah White 3 Feb.

1735.

Henry Penny & Charity Lowther 11 May

John Young & Elisabeth Street 29 May

Charles Hiscock & Mary Combs 17 July

Jonathan Roberts & Jane Penny 31 Aug.

1736.

William Penny & Martha Angood 2 May

Caleb Cavil & Tabitha Thomson 2 May

John Gold of Donhead St Andrew & Jane Mullens of Donhead St Mary 25 May

Matthew Pinnick & Mary Smith 20 June

Matthew Jay & Mary Anne Gold 9 July

Samuel Oak & Martha Martin 12 July

Shadrach Clements & Grace Humphrys of Braham 12 Aug.

John White & Elisabeth Masters both of Downhead 26 Sep.

John Merchant & Martha Russel 11 Oct.

1737.

Nicolas White & Hannah Strickland 17 Sep.

John Pin & Honour Gerard 20 Sep.

John Abbot of this Parish & Mary Hort of Martin 23 Nov.

1738.

George Gamblen of Tilshead & Mary
Yates 19 June
William Dean & Jane Dew 12 July
Robert Golding & Jane Stickland 3 Jan.
William Hertford & Mary Laws 4 Feb.

1739.

Philip Kirley & Martha Young 22 May
John Trimby & Ann Harcourt 12 Feb.

1740.

John Adams & Anne Gold 14 June
John Bryant & Anne Dupe 3 Aug.
Gyles Peckford & Martha Biggs 12 Aug.
Edmund Lush & Catharine Morris, both
of Martin, by Licence 14 Dec.
William Adlam & Susanna Savage 26 Dec.

1741.

William Meaden of Steeple Langford &
Anne Mould of Tisbury 4 Oct.

1742.

John Laws & Mary Bond 14 Nov.

1743.

Charles Silcock & Jane Harvey 11 July
Henry Coltman & Mary Barnes by Licence
16 Sep.
John Dibben & Mary Penny 6 Nov.

1744.

John Roaf & Jane Ingram 8 July
William Shepard & Mary Newman both
from Fordingbridge 11 Oct.

1745.

John Sturges & Sarah Viny 12 Nov.
William King & Elisabeth Harvey 24 Nov.
William Foyl & Mary Penny both of Burr
Chalk 10 Feb.

1746.

William James & Meilleure Angood 20
Sep.
David Gerard & Margaret Penn 28 Dec.

1747.

Thomas Burrough & Jane Foyl both of
Burr Chalk 27 April
Henry Herrington & Sarah Gold both of
Burr Chalk 15 June
Edward Presly of Compton & Mary
Ingram 25 June
Stephen Smith & Mary Archer 1 Oct.

John Grey & Jane Laws 3 Oct.
John Barter & Mary Marshal of Ebbsbourn 28 Dec.

1748.

John Brookman & Jane Barns 4 June
John Yates of Fifield & Anne Rolf 30
Sep.
William Stephens & Mary King 23 Jan.

1749.

William Haywood & Sarah Butcher 4
April
The Revd Mr John Bampton & Mrs Catha-
rine Eyre 3 July
Henry Young of Fifield & Jane Langtry
21 Aug.
Stephen Tanswell of Shafton & Jane
Young 1 Oct.
Moses Read & Anne Best 3 Oct.
William King & Elizabeth Merchant 21
Feb.

1750.

Nicolas Penny & Mary Carter both of
Bower Chalk 16 April
Robert Penny & Jane King 5 June
John Powel & Mary Strickland 2 Oct.
Matthew. Bleak & Sarah Read of Bower
Chalk 31 Oct.

1752.

John Batchelor of Bishopston & Mary
Gerard 20 May
Daniel Thompson & Betty Beling 28 June
Edward Hardiman & Ann Grey 28 Dec.

1753. N.S.

David Gerrard & Hannah Haskal 21 May
Thomas Teague & Alice Perry 4 Nov.
William Coles of Wimborn & Mary Framp-
ton of Bower Chalk 3 Dec.

1754.

Josiah Gould & Rebecca Harford 10 Jan.
Anthony Ingram & Mary Biggs 24 Feb.
*Thomas Cook & Elizabeth Scammel 23
July
William James & Mary Hayward 19 Aug.

1755.

William Foyl of Bower Chalk & Mary
Stainer 19 May
William Shepherd & Elizabeth Jollif 24
Aug.

* First entry in *printed* Register.

John Wilkins of Compton Chamberlain & Mary King 21 Sep.
Henry King & Jane King of Bower Chalk 11 Oct.

1756.

John Street & Susanna Combes 16 Oct.
John Foyl & Mary Noise 19 Oct.
William Penny & Elizabeth Knight 1 Nov.
John Lodge & Betty Stevens 15 Dec.

1757.

James Dean & Mary Turner 10 Feb.
William Brewer of Long Critchel, Dorset, & Rachael Hibberd 28 Oct.
William Beach of Fern Ditch (extra parochial) & Ann Griffin of the same place 25 Oct.
Thomas Trowbridge & Judith Reade 5 Dec.

1758.

John Stephens & Mary Vincent 5 Feb.
John Gray & Grace Hunt 12 Nov.

1759.

Samuel Foyl of Bower Chalk & Sarah Saunders 24 April
David Long & Sarah Penny 2 May
William Penny & Robina Witt 5 June
John Hibberd & Mary Young of Wilton 28 June
Thomas Foyle & Elizabeth Ingram 26 Dec.

1760.

John Haskel & Ann Lawes 14 July
George Reade & Susanna Roberts of Bishopston 16 Oct.
Richard Read of Bower Chalk & Jane Penny 9 Nov.
Henry Penny & Elizabeth Moody 18 Dec.

1761.

John Burton & Jane Gould 30 March
William Rowden of Steeple Langford & Hannah Lawes 13 April
Giles Quintin of Downton & Martha Powel 10 May
Henry Penny & Martha Gibbs 8 July
William Humby & Martha Folliot 26 Sep.
John Pinn & Mary Saunders 10 Oct.
David Penny & Martha Piercy 15 Oct.
William Whithorn of Stapleford & Aimée Harvy 15 Oct.
John Woodlands of Ebbesbourn & Ann Angood 5 Dec.

1762.

Richard Burrough & Mary Gould 23 June
John Yates & Mary Stocky 6 July

1763.

John Smart of Cranborne, Dorset, & Mary Brazier 14 Aug.
William Powell & Sarah Pinn 14 Dec.
John Cook & Ruth Smith 16 Dec.

1764.

John Johnson & Elizabeth Parret 30 Jan.
Raynold Randoll & Hannah Bowden 6 March
James Barter & Sarah Wilkins 24 April
William Lush & Sarah Folliot 29 Oct.
Stephen Smith & Mary Vincent, widow, 5 Nov.

1765.

William Wright & Mary Penny 29 April
Robert Golden & Jane Frampton of Bower Chalk 7 May
John Gould & Betty Witt 28 Oct.

1766.

William King & Mary Ingram 18 Jan.
John Fiefield & Elizabeth Goodson, widow, 1 April

1767.

James Willis of Stratford & Sarah King 9 Feb.
John Green & Ann Wilmot, widow, 8 Sep.

1768.

Edward Chub & Sarah Gibbs 4 July

1769.

John Bennett & Mary Hasell 4 Jan.
Joshua Dixon & Frances Humby of Cranbourn 8 Jan.
William Vitridge & Susan Vincent 4 June
Richard Folliot & Ann Saunders 16 Nov.
Love Bungey & Betty King 13 Dec.
John Cox & Mary Flooks of Chilton, Somerset, 17 Dec.

1770.

William Foyle & Mary Philips 5 May
William Hulet & Hannah Stocky 7 May
William Langtry & Mary Perry 5 June
Nicolas Flooks of Bishopstone & Jane Russel 18 June
Joseph Perry & Mary Powel 8 July
George Ingram & Mary Antram 8 Oct.

1771.

Henry Foot & Betty Sutton of Compton Chamberlain 17 Jan.

Robert Golden of Bower Chalk & Betty Andrews 8 April

Thomas Lass of Combe & Cassandra Jay 28 April

John Cerly & Elizabeth Hassel 28 July

Ambrose Loader & Betty Tompson 5 Aug.

Thomas Goasney & Elizabeth Frances 27 Oct.

Charles Read & Mary Parrot 9 Nov.

Philip Hiscock of Burford & Rebecca Hayden 20 Nov.

Samuel Parret & Sarah Ball 21 Nov.

1772.

John Morris & Lucy Barter 28 June

1773.

John Golden & Rebecca Webb of Handly 5 July

Stephen Jay & Sarah Haskell 19 Aug.

1774.

Elias Read & Martha Hayden 3 March

William Chub & Anne Bowles 28 May

1775.

James Diben & Anne Everet 17 July

Edward Musel & Sarah Viney of Bower Chalk 1 Aug.

George Hewlet & Rebecca Penny 16 Oct.

Robert Soffe of Vernditch Lodge, Extra parochial, & Mary Gifford 23 Nov.

1776.

James Smart & Betty Miles 16 April

John Batchelor & Mary Penn 8 July

John Jay & Mary Tompson 28 Oct.

William Langtry & Mary Tudgy 26 Nov.

John Goodfellow of Fovent & Jane Everret 27 Nov.

1777.

John Johnson of Bishopston & Mary Jay 5 Feb.

James Hillier & Sarah Jackmin 4 April

William Evans, clerk, & Mary Good, widow, 17 July

John Jeret & Hannah Ingram 12 Oct.

George Read & Anne Nash 23 Oct.

Joseph Emm & Elizabeth Langtry 13 Nov.

1778.

Stephen Barter of Bishopston & Elizabeth Barns 1 June

William Uphill of Barford & Deborah Gould 31 Aug.

1779.

Thomas Ford of Fovant & Mary Small 14 Jan.

John King of Fifield & Sarah Sanger 18 Oct.

1780.

William Feltham & Anne Emm 5 Feb.

Thomas Frances & Sarah Foyle 1 May

William Jay & Mary Church 14 June

Edward Mussel & Mary Cooke 3 July

Thomas Plowman of West Dean & Jane Gifford 24 Aug.

James Briant & Elizabeth Emm 17 Sep.

John Emm & Jane Scamel of Fovant 12 Oct.

Thomas Parsons of Dinton & Mary Dowland 16 Oct.

John Antram & Mary Huff 23 Nov.

Daniel Cavel & Sarah Coox 10 Dec.

APPENDIX,

BEING SUCH ENTRIES FROM THE MISSING REGISTERS AS ARE TO BE FOUND
IN THE DIOCESAN REGISTRY.

BIRTHS.

1658.
John s. John Stockey Junr 19 July
Edward s. Edward Osman 12 Sep.
Susnah d. George Acklen 8 Oct.
Tho. s. Christopher Penny 30 Nov.
Mary d. John Skiner 13 Dec.
Anne d. Tho. Benet 5 Jan.
Jeramiah s. Jeramiah Northest 13 Jan.
Elizabeth d. ffrances Hemor 11 Feb.
Andrew s. Andrew Deane 13 Feb.
Anna d. John White 13 March

1659.
Richard s. Richard Goold 15 July
Anthony s. Anthony Lodge 22 Sep.
Susanah d. Henry Quinten 22 Sep.
Mary d. Nicholas Nott 12 Dec.
Mary d. Mr Will. Grove 16 Dec.
Samuall s. Samuall Kinge 3 Jan.
Joane d. John Bundy 31 Jan.
Jane d. Richard Spencer 19 Jan.
Mary d. Robt Jaffery 18 Jan.
John s. Henry Penny 7 Feb.
Allexander s. Allexander Randoll 14 Feb.
Elizabeth d. Anthony Angood 14 Feb.

1660.
John s. Edward Osmand 19 April
Tho. s. Tho. Gilberd 27 March
Allice d. Robt Kinge 23 April
Will. s. Nicholas ffrances 14 May
Elizabeth d. Anthony Randoll 15 May
Katherine White d. Henry White 29 June
Tho. s. Roger Evens 24 Oct.
Tho. s. Will. Odber 22 Nov.
Henry s. Henry Penn 16 Dec.
John s. Walter Gray 17 Dec.
Arther s. Arther Brookman 28 Dec.
Anna d. Richard Wagge 17 Jan.
Sarah d. John Cooper 2 Feb.
Will. s. John Haris 20 Feb.
Mary d. Michall Huntly 16 Feb.
Anna d. Richard Spinser 22 Feb.
Avis d. Tho. Reade 28 Feb.

Edward s. John Penny 10 Mar.
ffrancis s. Edward Bidlecomb 24 March

1661.
Tho. s. Tho. Bates 26 Mar.
Henry s. Anthony Archer 15 April
Sarah d. Edward Brine 15 April
Jane d. John White 2 June
Bartholume s. Will. Kinge 6 May
Sarah d. Andrew Peane 28 July
Will. Simons s. Will. Simons 1 Sep.
Rose d. Tho. Bennet 22 Oct.
Mary d. George Antrum 24 Nov.
Elizabeth d. Anthony Penny 12 Jan.
John s. Mr Will. Grove 14 Jan.
Anthony s. Anthony Angood 21 Feb.

1662.
Anna d. Samuall Kinge 1 April
John s. Christopher Baker 20 April
Anna d. Henry Penny 4 May
Edward s. Edward Savedge 11 May
Anne d. John Stockey 11 May
Eideth d. Nicholas Nott 19 Oct.
Thomas s. Tho. Lovell 2 Nov.
Jane d. Rich. Orchard 2 Nov.
Rebeckah d. Christopher Penny 5 Nov.
John s. Anthony Randoll 9 Nov.
Mary d. Edward Brine 16 Nov.
Will. s. Will. Lodge 7 Dec.
Jane d. Henry White 21 Dec.
Rebeckah d. Phillip Bennet 27 Dec.
Avis d. Tho. Bates 28 Dec.
Katharen d. John Haris 13 Feb.
Anne d. Tho. Gilberd 22 Feb.
John s. John Penny 8 Mar.
John s. Roger Evens 8 Mar.

1663.
Grace d. Edward Osmond 5 April
Anne d. Tho. Browne 9 April
John s. Andrew Deane 12 April
Elizabeth d. George Acklen 14 June
Elizabeth d. Henry Watkenson 26 July
Abraham s. John White 4 Oct.

Mary d. Rob* Kinge 17 Jan.
Davidd s. Will. Smith 28 Feb.
Anna d. Walter Gray 28 Feb.

1664.

Elizabeth d. Edward Bidlecomb 8 April
Mary d. Richard Wagge 22 May
Elizabeth d. Allexander Randoll 12 June
Davidd s. M* Will. Grove 4 Sep.
Mary d. Samuall Kinge 18 Sep.
John s. Richard Spencer 22 Oct.
Tho. s. Tho. Penny 17 Nov.
Sarah d. George Antrum 30 Nov.
Will. s. Will. Andrew 18 Dec.
Mary d. Tho. Bates 9 Jan.
Ralphe s. Henry Penn 10 Jan.
Sarah d. Nicholas Nott 5 Feb.

1665.

John s. Robert Haillocke 27 Mar.
John s. Nicholas Minte 2 Ap.
Jane & Elizabeth twins of John Penny 17
    Ap.
Joane d. Phillip Bennet 30 Ap.
Richard s. Richard Aynell 5 June
Elizabeth d. John Haris 15 June
W^m s. Anthony Angood 22 June
Laurance s. Edmund Harvy 16 July
Jane d. Anthony Penny 8 Oct.
John s. Michall Huntly 10 Nov.
Mary d. W^m ffoxhanger 11 Nov.
George s. George Acklen 11 Nov.
Susanah d. Will. Andrew 10 Mar.
Rose d. Tho. Gilberd 12 Mar.
Joane d. Rob* Kinge 7 Mar.
Avis d. John White 19 Mar.

1666.

An d. Wm Carter 29 Mar.
Henry s. M* Will. Blanchard 30 Mar.
Anna d. Bartholmue Penny 16 April
Michall d. Will. Lodge 16 April
Will. s. Will. Marchent 16 April
Jane d. Will. Lawes 22 April
Garthred d. Ralphe Good 15 May
Mary d. Henry Watkenson 2 June
John s. Andrew Deane 2 July
Tho. s. Anthony Randoll 16 July
Jane d. Tho. Browne 15 Oct.
Charles s. John Stockey 24 Oct.
Nicholas s. Arther Brookman 28 Oc*.
Richard s. Walter Gray 29 Oct.
John s. John Streete 19 Nov.
Mary d. Tho. Penny 3 Dec.
Mary d. Richard Spencer 7 Dec.
Thos. Rich. Wagge 2 Feb.

Joane d. Tho. Bates 11 Feb.
Mary d. Davidd Earwood 18 Mar.

1667.

Deborah d. Samuall Kinge 8 April
Elizabeth d. Rob* Jaffery 23 April
Abigall d. Will. Smyth 1 May
George s. George Antrum 10 June
Sarah d. Richard Orchard 11 June
Richard s. John Penny 8 July
Phillip s. Phillip Bennet 28 July
Elizabeth d. Will. Neve 29 July
Joane d. Will. Prist 18 Aug.
Joyce d. Henry Penny 26 Aug.
Sibell d. Edward Osmond 13 Sep.
John s. Nicholas Nott 15 Sep.
Allexander s. Allexander ffrances 18 Oct.
Will. s. Will. Hutchens 6 Dec.
Jane d. Anthony Randoll 25 Feb.
Elizabeth d. Ralphe Good 24 Mar.

1668.

Jane d. Rob* Haillock 29 Mar.
Will. s. Will. ffoxhanger 30 Mar.
Will. s. Roger Evens 30 Ap.
John s. Wm Marchent 3 May
Jonathan s. George Acklen 22 May
Timothy s. Timothy Lodge 27 May
Anna d. John Witte 29 May
Sarah d. Rob* Kinge 8 June
John s. Tho. Gilberd 24 Sep.
John s. John ffrances 29 Oct.
Henry Watkenson 23 Dec.
Hester d. Andrew (? Deane) Peane 18 Jan.
Elizabeth d. John Goulding 1 Mar.
Anna d. Tho. Richards 18 Mar.

1669.

Elizabeth d. Davidd Earewood 12 April
Henry s. Walter Gray 31 May
Elizabeth d. John Street 19 June
John s. Anthony Angood 14 Sep.
Will. s. Tho. Penny 11 Oct.
Mary d. Henry Kinge 2 Nov.
Jane d. Bartholmue Penny 21 Nov.
Rich. s. Rich. Wagge 2 Dec.
Jane d. Edward Osmond 10 Dec.
Anna d. Anthony Randoll 13 Jan.
Mary d. Cornelius Shorte 23 Jan.
Jane d. Samuall Kinge 26 Jan.
Elizabeth d. George Antrum 27 Feb.
Anne d. Tho. Richards 24 Mar.

1670.

Will. s. Allexander ffrances *bap.* 28 Mar.
Mary d. John Penny 5 Ap.
Walter s. Phillip Bennet 8 May

Abigall d. Will. Marchent
Peregreene Dove, a wonderer, 12 June
Will. s. Henry Penny 3 Sep.
John s. Tho. Bats 3 Sep.
Allice, aged 11 yeares, d. George Overy 14 Sep.
John s. John Brine 24 Sep.

Dorothy d. Ralphe Good 6 Nov.
John s. Will. Hutchens 9 Dec.
Ann d. Will. Andrew 28 Dec.
Allice base borne d. Allice Penny 14 Feb.
Randoll s. Randoll Lodge 25 Feb.
Mary d. John ffrances 20 Mar.

BAPTISMS.

1671.
William s. Thomas Richards 29 April
Henry s. Henry King 22 May
Edith d. Wm Vincent 1 June
Thomas s. John Randoll 25 July
Elizabeth d. Wm Lawes 30 July
W^m s. John Penny 10 Aug.
Jane d. W^m ffox 20 Aug.
John s. George Lawes 6 Nov.
Mary d. John Street, jun^r 28 Nov.
Edward s. Phillip Bennett 27 Dec.
Elizabeth d. Andrew Deane 4 March

1672.
George Golden s. John 29 May
Thomas Richards s. Thomas 17 Jan.
Elizabeth Randol d. John 12 Sep.
Martha Penny d. Thomas 15 Sep.
George Marchant s. William 24 Sep.
Frances Crosse d. William 30 Sep.
Robert Wag s. Richard 1 Nov.
Elizabeth Tapper d. John 15 Jan.
Ann Odbur d. William 12 April

1673.
Denis Brine d. John 7 Sep.
Jane ffrancis d. John 21 Sep.
Jane King d. Henry 30 Sep.
William Randol s. Anthony 20 Nov.
Henry Randol s. John 9 Dec.
Joseph Hutchins s. William 11 Dec.
John Witt s. John 10 Feb.
John Stocky s. Thomas 26 Feb.
Timothy Lodge s. Randol 18 March

1674.
William Herford s. William 29 March
Margaret Penny d. John 12 April
Ann Whitmarsh d. Jasper 20 April
Ralphe s. John Boyter 20 May
Anne d. Avis White 6 June
John s. John Dunne 8 June
Ambrose s. Thomas Richards 1 July
Mary d. Phillip Bennet 28 July
John s. Alexander ffrancis 5 Aug.
William s. William Whitmarsh 9 Sep.

Joyce d. William Seager 22 Sep.
William s. William Bigs 30 Oct.
Catharine d. John Street 9 Nov.
John s. Robert Wit 10 Dec.
Mary d. John Follet 2 Feb.
Henry s. Henry Cook

1675.
Henry s. Henry Randoll 27 April
Jane d. Richard Mullins 29 May
Henry s. Ralph Good 25 June
Henry s. Henry Miles 3 July
Abigail d. Anthony Angood 19 Sep.
Henry s. Thomas Penny 23 Sep.
Christabel Harford d. William 3 Oct.
Jasper s. Jasper Whitmarsh 1 Nov.
Elizabeth d. Thomas Richards 29 Dec.
Elisabeth d. John Brine 29 Dec.
Jane d. John Randoll 5 Jan.
Thomas s. Thomas Fish 21 Jan.
Jasper s. William Merchant 1 Feb.
Thomas s. Andrew Deane 7 Feb.
Sarah d. William Biggs 11 March

*1696.
Ann Hasell
Joyce Penn
Ann Haylock
Henry Biddlecomb
John White
Edward Keed
Laurence Harvy
Sarah Goold
Richard Akland
Francis Miles
Mary Frances
Jane Penny
Edward Carter
Mary Lodge
Edith Norris
Mary Russel
Lucy Austen
Joseph Savage
Mary Fox

* No returns to be found for the interval between 1675—1696.—C. G. M.

MARRIAGES.

None between 1649 and 1653.

1653.

Nicholas Nott & Edith Mihell 28 Dec.
John Randoll & Edith Good 6 Jan.
Robert King & Anne King 27 Jan.
Robt Jeffery & Mary Moxham 2 Feb.
William Miles & Michaell Angood 7 Mar.
William Pitchland & Joyce Penny 20 Mar.

1654.

Richard Spenser & Jane Lodge 5 Feb.

1655.

Henry Penny & Allice Lodge 4 June
Arther Brookman & Joane Savidge 18 June
George Aiklem (?) & Mary Mullens 4 July

1656.

John Enred & Elizabeth Deane 5 May
Samuall King & Joane King 12 June
Charles Burden & Mary Mils 25 June
Anthony Randoll & Jane Noris 25 June
Allexander ffrances & Elizabeth Miles 27 Sep.
John White & Babarah King 15 Dec.
Will. Brine & Elizabeth Spiring 2 Feb.

1657.

Charles Newman & Eideth Northover 22 Sep.
George Northover & Ellinor Brine 29 Sep.

1658.

Walter Gray & Anne Mullens 26 April

1660.

William Carter & Mary Good 11 June
Tho. Lovell & Elizabeth Good 27 Sep.

1661.

George Antrum & Jane ffolliat 10 June
Bartholmue Penny & Margaret Deane 14 Jan.
Will. Lodge & Elizabeth Lawes 5 Feb.

1665.

Will. Lawes & Michall Good 3 April
John Good & Anna Geret 13 June

1666.

John ffrances & Mary Stockey 7 June
Will. Hutchens & Katherine Richardes 29 Nov.

1668.

Cornellius Shorte & Ellinor ffarent 30 Mar.
Tho. Richards & Ellinor Clarke 6 Aug.
George Acklen & Allis Huntle 23 Nov.

1669.

Mr Nicholas Grove & Mrs Abigale Sloper 18 July

1671.

ffrancis Deacon & Jane Bundy 7 Jan.

1672.

Mr James Bennet & Mrs Jane Saintloe 10 April
Thomas Penn & Anna Thomas 1 May
John Etsal & Dennis Whitmarsh 20 June
Robert Witt & Mary Bidlecomb 24 Nov.

1675.

Christopher Smith & Anne Penny 20 June
Thomas Fish & Elizabeth Harvy 24 June
Christopher Bush & Dorothy Orchard 25 Oct.

*1696.

Andrew Dew & Abigal Merchant
Nathaniel Bowne & Sarah Ford

1711.

Arthur Hopkins & Jane Whitmarsh 8 May

1712.

Robert Tyler of Crewkhorn & Michel Dew 21 July
William Chalk & Jone Francis 25 Sep.

1713.

Samuel Penny & Sarah Barter 18 April
Andrew Tapp of Barford & Mary Jefferies 30 July

* No returns to be found for the intervals between 1675—1696 and 1696—1711.—C. G. M.

George Creed & Hannah West both of
Sarum 5 Sep.

1716.

Thomas Fox of East Dean, Hants & Grace
Adlam 5 Nov.

1717.

William Lilly & Dinah Ingram 1 Aug.
Peregrine Dove & Mary Frampton 30
Sep.
John Lewin & Elizabeth Foster 29 Oct.
Edward Harvey & Mary Powell 10 Feb.
John Angood & Melior Burroughs 16
Feb.

1718.

Jasper Willis of Bishopston & Jane Mar-
tin 1 June
Thomas Viney & Margaret Elkyns 30
Sep.

1719.

Rinaldo Freke of Shafton & Martha Bundy 25 May
Anthony Penny & Jane Antram 15 July

Thomas Wilkins & Sarah Donne 14 Jan.
Samuel Penny & Ann Lush 15 Feb.

1721.

William Dawkins of Wilton & Elizabeth
Aynold of Bishopston 12 Oct.
John Burton of Ebbesborn & Joyce Has-
kel of Alvediston 25 Dec.
John Hiscock & Mary Lodge of Alvediston
7 Feb.

1722.

Jacob Jennings & Mary Fish 20 July
Thomas Street of Martin & Dorothy
Goold 1 Jan.

1724.

John Day & Ann Haylock 30 April
John Laws & Hannah Homar 26 May
Samuel Jeffreys & Mary Segar 10 June
George Antram & Ruth White 1 Oct.
Alexander Penny & Jane Harvey 1 Oct.
Simon Marks & Elizabeth King 22 Nov.
Edward Fisher & Ann Young 29 Nov.

1725.

Thomas King & Mary Angood 11 April
Edward Savage & Judith Savage 13 Feb.

BURIALS.

1654.

Will. s. John Skiner 27 March
Elizabeth w. Andrew Deane 9 April
Joane w. Will. Angood 11 May
Joane Scud w. Tho. Scud 8 Aug.
Will. s. Allexander King 9 Dec.
Allice w. Robt Whitmarsh 18 Jan.
Hannah d. Tho. Holly 20 Feb.

1655.

Jane d. John Pringe 27 March
John s. Robt Randoll 26 April
Will. Spiring of Stoake 10 June
Anis w. Walter Newman 29 Nov.
Garthred d. Henry Good 20 Dec.
John s. Will. Lawes 15 Jan.

1656.

Moses s. John Bundy 7 May
Margaret d. Will. King 7 June
Tho. s. John Skamell 24 June
Cornelius Miles of Stooke 18 July
Barbarah w. Will. Andrew 13 Nov.
Robt s. John King 16 Jan.
Elizabeth d. Allex. Randoll 31 Jan.
Mary d. John Sanders 19 March

1657.

Abigall w. Mr John Sloper 9 April
Jane w. Henry Laurence 16 May
Anna w. Charles Newman 30 May
Will. Angood 31 May
Walter Newman 15 July
Elizabeth d. Nicholas Savidg 24 July
John s. Samuall Lisle 1 Aug.
Tho. s. Edward Bidlecomb 14 Sep.
Anne Lodge 5 Oct.
Elizabeth ffrances 5 Oct.
Elizabeth Angood, widow, 25 Oct.
John s. Henry Good de Moulson 2 Nov.
Margaret w. Samuall Lisle 5 Nov.
Henry Good de Moulson 9 Dec.
Daniall s. Will. Peane 16 Dec.
Will. s. Daniall Peane 29 Dec.
Solloman s. Solloman Penny 24 Jan.
Ellianor Brine, widow, 16 Feb.
Mary d. Mr Will. Grove 20 Feb.
Michall d. John Lawes 23 Feb.
Widow Webbe de Moulson 2 March

1658.

Laurence Saintloe, gent, 26 April
Mathew Perry 27 April

Will. Whitmarsh 28 April
Jane d. Mr Will. Grove 9 May
Henry s. Henry Good Senr de Moulson 26 May
Walter s. Edward Bennet 27 May
John d. (sic) Henry Randoll 14 June
Will. Archer, sen^r, 17 July
Tho. s. Tho. Pen 11 Aug.
Walter s. Richard Wagge 15 Aug.
Tho. Ploweman 14 Sep.
Mr Younge s. of Younge of ffifeld 25 Sep.
Katharine d. Cornelius Witte 28 Sep.
Mary d. Cornelius Witte 7 Oct.
Rebecka d. Cornelius Witte 18 Oct.
Christian Miles w. Ralphe Miles 23 Oct.
Anthony s. Anthony Archer 31 Oct.
Elizabeth w. John Smyth 6 Jan.
Brighteeweed w. Tho. Selwood 6 Jan.
Elizabeth King, widow, 8 Jan.
Tho. Randoll, in the Greene 14 Jan.
Solloman Penny de Stoake 16 Jan.
Elizabeth w. John Blake 22 Jan.
Mary Prist alias Simons 30 Jan.
Robt Ledford 7 Feb.
Anne d. Mr John Sloper 9 Feb.
Anna w. Gabrell Kinge 20 March
Henry Lawes of Apsshill 26 Jan.

1659.

Mary ffrances of Knighton 16 April
Michall w. Robt Ledford 18 May
Rich. s. Christopher Baker 22 June
John s. Will. Savidge 5 Nov.
John Nott of Knighton 19 Dec.
Diones Scud alias Gilberd w. Tho. Gilberd 12 Feb.
Henry Thome of Stoake 3 March

1660.

Joane w. Bartholmue Segar 13 July
Bartholmue s. Bartho. Segar 29 July
Mary w. Ralphe Penn 31 Aug.
Nicholas Savage 21 Sep.
Will. Michell alias Thrasher 26 Sep.

1717.

Anthony Perry 2 April
Thomas s. Thomas Penny 22 April
John Francis 26 April
Martha w. J. Marshall of Bishopston 21 May
Ann w. Peregrine Dove 8 June
Joan Bennet, widow, 4 July
Esther Cook, widow, 7 July

Ann Odber, widow, 17 July
Annabella Stockey, widow, 19 July
Edward s. Wm Chalk 22 Aug.
William Andrews 3 Sep.
Margaret Ann d. Willm Wray 9 Sep.
Lucy Angood 21 Nov.
Mary d. Thomas Young 19 Jan.
John s. John Littlefield 31 Jan.
Jane d. John Littlefield 12 Feb.
Mary Odber, widow, 12 Feb.
John Odber 10 March
Joyce w. Willm Seager 18 March
John Lawes 23 March

1718.

Henry King 20 April
Henry s. Henry King 20 May
Joseph s. Henry Randol 24 May
Joyce Marchant, widow, 29 May
Mary d. Henry Randol 6 June
Mary Watkins, widow, 7 June
Charles Miles 16 Aug.

Joan King, widow, 23 Sep.
Richard s. Samuel Penny 23 Sep.
Thomas Randol 30 Sep.
William s. Willm Lilly 9 Oct.
Walter s. Walter Whitmarsh 28 Feb.
Jasper Whitmarsh 7 March

1719.

Nicholas Savage 18 April
Martha w. Willm Harford 2 May
George s. Laurence Brookman 6 June
Elizabeth d. Richd Hawkins 27 Aug.
Bartholomew King of Fifield 10 Sep.
Ruth d. Thomas Penny 22 Oct.
Elizabeth w. John Elderton of Bishopston
    1 Nov.
Elizabeth King of Fifield, widow, 5 Nov.
Martha d. Willm Speering 6 Nov.
Ambrose Richards 11 Dec.
John Ingram 25 Dec.
Elizabeth King, widow, 23 March

INDEX.

London : Mitchell and Hughes, Printers, 140 Wardour Street, W.

www.ingramcontent.com/pod-product-compliance
Lightning Source LLC
LaVergne TN
LVHW051125190726
843642LV00003B/622